Mexico's Supreme Court

MEXICO'S SUPREME COURT

Between Liberal Individual and Revolutionary Social Rights, 1867–1934

Timothy M. James

University of New Mexico Press
Albuquerque

Printed in the United States of America
18 17 16 15 14 13 1 2 3 4 5 6

Library of Congress Cataloging-in-Publication Data

James, T. M. (Timothy M.)
Mexico's Supreme Court : between liberal individual rights and revolutionary social rights, 1867–1934 / Timothy M. James.
pages cm
Includes bibliographical references and index.
ISBN 978-0-8263-5378-8 (cloth : alk. paper) — ISBN 978-0-8263-5379-5 (electronic)
1. Mexico—Suprema Corte de Justicia—History. 2. Constitutional courts—Mexico—History. 3. Civil rights—Mexico—History. 4. Social rights—Mexico—History. 5. Mexico—Politics and government—1867–1910. 6. Mexico—Politics and government—1910–1946. I. Title.
KGF2530.J345 2014
347.72'03509034—dc23
2013011565

BOOK DESIGN: Catherine Leonardo
Composed in 10.25/13.5 Minion Pro Regular
Display type is Italian Old Style MT Std Regular

For my parents, Tim and Terri James

Contents

Acknowledgments

This book, a history of constitutional rights and their judicial interpretation by Mexico's Supreme Court from the Restored Republic to the Maximato, could not have been written without access to the Supreme Court's historical archive. I am indebted to Jorge Flores for providing this access and to his staff for locating hard to find materials and providing me with a space to work. I was also aided by the librarians and archivists of four other institutions—the Procuraduría General de la República, the Escuela Libre de Derecho, the Archivo General de la Nación, and the Biblioteca Central "Silvestre Moreno Cora"—whose collections were indispensable for the research that went into this book. In addition, I would like to thank Norma Mereles de Ogarrio for granting me access to the Fideicomiso Archivos Plutarco Elías Calles y Fernando Torreblanca in Mexico City. I would also like to thank Linda Arnold and Alejandro Mayagoitia, knowledgeable scholars in the field of Mexican legal history who generously shared with me their private collections and considerable knowledge of Mexican law.

I owe a special debt of gratitude to the late Friedrich Katz, whose memory lives on in all of those who had the pleasure of working with him. My own interpretation of the Mexican Revolution has very much been shaped by his two histories of the Mexican Revolution—*The Secret War* and *The Life and Times of Pancho Villa*—as well as a third book project on the Revolutionary leader Francisco Madero, which Friedrich's untimely death in 2010 prevented him from finishing. I would also like to thank Kif Agustine-Adams, Luis Barron, Dain Borges, Jeffrey Bortz, Elizabeth Borgwardt, Carlos Bravo, Jason

Dawsey, Michael Geyer, Charles Hale, Elizabeth Heath, Tamar Herzog, Susan Karr, Emilio Kouri, Mark Loeffler, Spencer Leonard, Claudio Lomnitz, Graciela Márquez, Everard Meade, Pablo Mijangos, William Novak, Alejandra Núñez Luna, Sarah Osten, Moishe Postone, Peter Reich, Colby Ristow, Paul Ross, Michael Scardeville, Ana María Serna, William H. Sewell Jr., Andrew Sloin, Laura Sour, Rob Stern, William Suarez-Potts, Paul Townend, Seoneid Valient, and Reuben Zahler. The usual caveats apply and I assume ultimate responsibility for any errors of fact or interpretation that the reader may find herein. Nonetheless, this book would have been a very different and less interesting work without the input from so many gifted scholars and mentors.

An earlier version of chapters 2, 3, and 4 was published by Mexico's Supreme Court in 2010 as *Revolución social e interpretación constitucional: La Suprema Corte y las reformas sociales revolucionarias, 1916–1934*. An earlier version of chapter 1 was published as "Derecho constitucional y el juicio de amparo durante el Porfiriato" in the multiauthored volume *De Cádiz al siglo XXI: Doscientos años de constitucionalismo en México e Hispanoamérica (1812–2012)*, published by Taurus/CIDE in 2012. An earlier version of chapter 3 first appeared in English in *Law and History Review*, published by the University of Illinois Press, and I gratefully acknowledge their permission to use that material here.

For both his interest and help in preparing the final manuscript for publication, I would like to thank Clark Whitehorn of the University of New Mexico Press. Thanks also goes to Joy Margheim, Robert Landrum, and Carl Eby, all of whom read and commented on the final draft, as did Darby James, who has shared and lived with this project in all of its many incarnations. It would certainly never have been completed without her patience and understanding. My department chair at the University of South Carolina Beaufort, Babet Villena-Alvarez, supported this book with travel funds and course-release time. Questions related to Spanish translation were ably fielded by Leonor Teves Taylor. Research for this book was also generously funded by the Mellon Foundation. The debt I owe my parents for their support in this project as well as so many others can hardly be summarized here. It seems more than appropriate, especially as I look forward to the birth of my own first son, to dedicate this book to them.

Introduction

Mexico is not a country well known for its tradition of constitutional jurisprudence, and the Porfiriato, in particular, is considered a period when constitutional-rights protections on the books were systematically ignored in practice. Nonetheless, it was during the last third of the nineteenth century that a system of constitutional procedures protecting liberal individual rights—known in Spanish as *amparo*—was firmly established for the first time in Mexican constitutional law. This system was suspended for several years during the Mexican Revolution, was reincorporated largely unchanged into a new Revolutionary constitution in 1917, and was to have important consequences for the implementation of new socioeconomic rights in the period from 1917 to 1934.

The Constitution of 1917 is best known for these new social rights, specifically the agrarian and labor provisions to be found in articles 27 and 123. Article 27 protected the right to property but established new limits, including the need to "divide large landed estates" and provide land for the landless.[1] Article 123 created a set of far-reaching protections for workers and their families, including a mandated day of rest, minimum-wage provisions, employer liability for work accidents, the recognition of unions, and the right to strike. Indeed, there is not a single history of the Mexican Revolution that has not weighed in on the question of the relationship of articles 27 and 123 to the legitimacy of the new Revolutionary regime.

If in this respect this book—which also takes up the question of articles 27 and 123—traverses well-traveled ground, it nonetheless aims to offer fresh insights through the adoption of a new perspective, that of

Mexican legists deciding and litigating constitutional cases. Its main innovation over previous accounts, then, is its use of jurisprudential sources—that is, the resolutions of federal tribunals, as well as the writings and commentaries of jurists and other legal professionals. This shift in source base allows for a new interpretation of Mexico's Revolutionary Constitution of 1917 and the history of socioeconomic rights in particular.

The critique implicit in a turn to jurisprudence, then, is that other accounts that have taken up the topic of the Constitution's social rights have focused exclusively on legislation (and the legislature) and have ignored judicial sources. The costs of this neglect have been substantial. Because historians have conceived of law almost exclusively in terms of legislation, they have failed to appreciate the many ways in which legal changes brought about by judicial interpretation have been concealed by legislative continuities, or they have failed to register the way continuities in judicial interpretation could present an obstacle to the implementation of new legislation. Yet both of these dynamics were at work with respect to Mexico's Revolutionary social rights from 1917 until 1934.

The most important English-language work that focuses on the constitutionalization of new socioeconomic rights is E. V. Niemeyer's classic study *Revolution at Querétaro: The Mexican Constitutional Convention of 1916–1917.* Although Niemeyer stops his study in 1917, other histories of the Mexican Revolution have increasingly made it a habit to push beyond 1917, to either 1920 or 1924 (or even 1940). These studies have not only addressed the question posed by Niemeyer of constitutional change legislated by the Constituent Congress, but they have also sought to assess the problem of the Constitution's halting and partial implementation—at least prior to the acceleration of socioeconomic reforms under President Lázaro Cárdenas (1934–1940)—by suggesting several barriers to implementation. These have included such barriers as coordination problems at the federal and local levels, the failure of the legislature to pass much-needed legislation regulating new rights, the social conservatism of executive-branch leadership, especially under President Venustiano Carranza (1917–1920), and finally international pressures, above all, U.S. imperialism.[2] However, none of these studies have mentioned the role of the federal judicial power in this regard and they have generally ignored changes in constitutional jurisprudence.

Indeed, of the major works of synthesis that have appeared in the past thirty-five years, including Adolfo Gilly's *The Mexican Revolution*, John Hart's *Revolutionary Mexico*, and Alan Knight's *The Mexican Revolution*, only

Ramón Ruíz's *The Great Rebellion* mentions by name amparo (literally, "protection")—that is, the power of the federal judiciary to nullify unconstitutional acts and laws—as a barrier to the implementation of Revolutionary social reform.[3] Ruíz's confusion over the details of amparo procedure and its constitutional basis, however, underscores the dearth of research in the area of Mexico's judicial institutions. These include his claim that amparo was "[a] legal precept dating from the Decree of January 6, 1915" and the idea that "the entire lineup of federal courts," including, presumably, federal circuit courts, was involved in amparo proceedings, an error shared by more recent work on the nineteenth century as well.[4] But these errors, understandable given the state of the field, are a significant problem because the technical legal rules of constitutional rights enforcement are crucial for an understanding of the meaning and practice of constitutional law and constitutional rights.[5] Some of these rules, it is true, can be deduced from a study of legislation alone, but the study of formal rules is just the tip of the proverbial iceberg, for reasons specific to amparo's nineteenth- and early twentieth-century history.[6]

Thus it is hardly surprising that the tendency of historians (and many legal scholars as well) to reduce the study of the law to just one of its sources (i.e., legislation), has resulted in a glaring blind spot in the literature on the Mexican Revolution—namely, the Supreme Court's role in obstructing the implementation of socioeconomic rights.[7] Hence the main questions this book seeks to answer: how, why, and when exactly did the Supreme Court's interpretation of the Constitution become a barrier to the implementation of state-level labor legislation and agrarian land rights between 1917 and 1934?

One possible answer to the above questions is that federal judges and Supreme Court justices were ideologically opposed to the redistributive social principles contained in the Constitution. This was certainly the answer proposed at the time by agrarians such as Antonio Díaz Soto y Gama and many of the leaders of the urban working classes. It has remained one of the predominant explanations in the literature on labor law.[8] It is also the explanation provided by Ruíz. "At the close of the years of revolutionary rhetoric," writes Ruíz, "whatever the gains of laws and constitutional statutes pledging to revamp the pattern of land ownership, the landless only marginally savored victory." One important reason for this was that "the enemies of social change"—that is, large landowners and others with a vested interest in the status quo—now had recourse to the courts, and this "quickly put a brake on land reform." The social conservatism of Supreme Court justices and federal district judges during this period only made matters worse. "[T]he Chief

Justice of the Supreme Court was far from impartial, urging [President Alvaro] Obregón in 1922 to halt the granting of land on a provisional basis," and "the Juez de Distrito [district judge] was not uncommonly a friend of the *hacendado* [owner of a large estate], and his judgment often reflected it."[9]

Certainly the fact that between 1917 and 1934 the Mexican Supreme Court granted hundreds of amparos favoring industrialists and landowners against the interests of the urban and rural lower classes appears to support these and similar characterizations. In this respect the Mexican case appears strikingly similar to a pattern and a dynamic that took place elsewhere at about the same time. Although the first to raise socioeconomic rights to the level of constitutional law, Mexico was not the only country where judicial opposition to social legislation and its implementation had profound legal and political effects. In the United States, for example, the U.S. Supreme Court adopted an interpretation of the U.S. Constitution's Fourteenth Amendment known as "economic substantive due process," on which it based its opposition to state-level labor laws like maximum-hours legislation and other kinds of regulatory laws in the name of contractual freedom. According to Justice Oliver Wendell Holmes in his famous dissent in *Lochner v. New York* (1905), this use of the Fourteenth Amendment was tantamount to incorporating the economic theory of laissez-faire into the Constitution.[10] To this day *Lochner* remains "shorthand in constitutional law for the worst sins of subjective judicial activism."[11] And the logic of the *Lochner* decision "made the Court the overseer of all kinds of state regulatory legislation. Between 1905 and 1937 when the Court rejected this rationale in *West Coast Hotel v. Parrish* (1937), countless subsequent attempts to reform social and economic conditions were challenged on the precedent of *Lochner*."[12] In the 1930s the U.S. Supreme Court nullified significant portions of Franklin Delano Roosevelt's New Deal, leading to a backlash against the Court that culminated in Roosevelt's famous "Court-packing plan." Although Roosevelt's plan failed, it very well could have succeeded, as did a similar plan approved in Mexico in 1928. Thus judicial interpretation of the U.S. Constitution during this period put a brake on progressive social legislation and was widely regarded at the time to have required a politically motivated reinterpretation of certain liberal individual rights with profound antimajoritarian implications.

A similar account of judicial power favoring vested economic interests in the face of social democratic reforms has been told for Germany during the period of the Weimar Republic (1919–1933). Obviously, Germany's constitutional tradition was different from both Mexico's and the United States'. Germany was similar to Mexico in that its legal system was rooted in the civil law traditions of continental Europe. Unlike the United States and Mexico, however, Germany did not have a nineteenth-century tradition of judicial control of federal legislation. Nonetheless, the Weimar Constitution of 1919 created for the first time the institution of a constitutional court, which, throughout the Weimar period, asserted its ability to review the constitutionality of both state (land) and federal laws.[13] Like the U.S. judiciary, German judges expanded the meaning of certain individual rights, notably the equality clause to be found in constitutional article 109. They also expanded the meaning of the right to property, subsuming new kinds of government acts and new kinds of property (now treated as a "bundle of rights") under the "takings clause" of constitutional article 153.[14] According to the historian Peter Caldwell, "[T]hese shifts [in judicial interpretation] often corresponded to a conservative political position, which . . . seemed to want to limit the power of the democratic legislature against the intentions of the constitution's founders."[15]

Was this also the case in Mexico? In part, but as the legal literature on amparo has also noted, the direction of (judge-made) legal change often favored Revolutionary social reform.[16] To the extent that both the direction and the timing of these changes are correct, then, something more than just an ideological gap between the judiciary and the legislative branch or executive needs to be explained. Moreover, no expansion of the scope of judicial control over the other powers was "legislated" by the Mexican judiciary in the manner usually described for Germany and the United States, and it seems likely that the Mexican judiciary was not as ideologically opposed to the new social rights as has sometimes been supposed. This is not to say that politics and conservative (or, more properly speaking, liberal) ideologies did not play their part. Nor does this mean that changes in past precedent and judge-made law did not take place. It is to say, however, that innovations in judge-made law were ultimately in a "social" (or Revolutionary) not a "liberal" (or conservative) direction and these aided in the loosening of the Supreme Court's previous jurisdictional controls over the legality and constitutionality of government acts and laws. One of the main arguments of this book is that this fact cannot simply be explained away with recourse to the alleged weakness or nonexistence of a Mexican tradition of judicial control or to the alleged subservience of the Mexican judiciary to the executive power. On the contrary, it is precisely the existence and importance of this tradition of judicial control historically and the relative degree of autonomy exercised by the judiciary during this period that must be grappled with and illuminated if we are to understand this process and the crisis of an independent judicial power later in the twentieth century.

The argument proceeds as follows. Chapter 1 provides background on the procedural rules and enforcement of liberal individual rights by the federal judicial power prior to 1910. It discusses the amparo principles themselves, their relation to other aspects of Mexico's constitutional tradition, and the two most litigated articles of constitutional-rights adjudication, articles 14 and 16. Chapter 2 picks up the story in 1910. It addresses the question of the legislative changes brought about by the Revolution, especially with respect to constitutional law. The most important of these changes were obviously those legislated by the Constituent Congress of 1916–1917. However, these changes must be viewed in the context of a lived tradition of constitutional law (a fact often obscured by Revolutionary historiography) as well as the larger political changes that the Revolution wrought. This chapter also seeks to explain how a revolution that began in the name of political rights to effective suffrage (and a platform of no reelection) ended by constitutionalizing socioeconomic rights, the first of their kind. Chapter 3 traces the early history of Mexico's Supreme Court as it was reconstituted after 1917 but with a specific focus on its interpretation of article 123's socioeconomic rights favoring the working class. It shows how past precedent and a previous interpretation of the division of powers led the Court to become a major obstacle to the implementation of the new labor law. The chapter ends in 1924 with the Supreme Court's jurisprudential creation of administrative tribunals, an innovation that was interpreted at the time as a victory for the working class. Chapter 4 picks up where chapter 3 left off but switches the focus from the labor provisions to the implementation of article 27's agrarian reform provisions. Here, too, the Court became an obstacle to the implementation of redistributive social rights. Nonetheless, the chapter argues that the Court's jurisprudence on this question should not be characterized as an expansion of judicial power in defense of vested landed interests. Eventually amparo itself would be suspended in agrarian matters, and this, along with other legal changes that broke with an older paradigm of nineteenth-century public law, can be seen as a necessary precondition for the oft-cited acceleration of social reform during the *sexenio* of President Cárdenas.

CHAPTER ONE

The Judicial Protection of Constitutional Rights during the Porfiriato

> When the historians of the future study carefully our epoch and calmly and philosophically judge the complex causes of our interior peace and our growing material progress, they will take into account, without doubt, the energy with which the administration has squashed with an iron fist the first hints of rebellion: but they will also have to take into account that if the pacification of the country has operated to a significant extent it has been, among other important factors, because the amparo suit has permitted, in general, the reparation of an infinity of arbitrary acts, whose effects, without doubt, would have used up, sooner or later, the patience and abnegation of the Mexican people.
>
> —Miguel Bolaños Cacho, 1908

The Porfiriato as a historical period has long been viewed from the perspective of Mexico's social revolution of 1910. This is no doubt a testament to the scale and scope of the conflagration itself, which intensified and radicalized after 1913 and did not come to an end until at least 1917 but more conventionally 1920, or (with recourse to the notion of a long "Thermidor" between 1917 and 1934) perhaps not until 1940.[1] The events that unfolded after 1910 were by and large unprecedented in the history of Latin America despite the region's reputation for revolutionary upheavals.[2] After thirty years of relative political stability consolidated around the shrewd politician and celebrated military hero of the French Intervention, Gen. Porfirio Díaz, the country was plunged into a civil war whose outcome could not have been predicted by anyone in 1910, least of all by those most acquainted with Mexican affairs.[3] It would eventually lead to the raising of large Revolutionary armies capable of engaging and defeating federal troops in battles fought along conventional lines. These Revolutionary armies then turned on each other. By 1921, after a little more than a decade of civil war, bullets, disease, and food shortages had combined to kill or displace from Mexican territory more than eight hundred thousand people.[4] It is hardly surprising, then, that the historical problem of the Porfirian peace, or Pax Porfiriana, alluded to in the quotation by Miguel Bolaños Cacho, has been eclipsed by the question of the Revolution's Porfirian antecedents and causes. Perhaps for this reason, too, amparo, contrary to Bolaños's pre-Revolutionary expectations, has been little studied by historians.

This is not to say that constitutional law has not been implicated in a causal account of the Revolution. It surely has. However, many of these accounts leave much to be desired and they have been limited in their conclusions by a neglect of constitutional jurisprudence. Indeed, the vast majority of these accounts have tended to repeat the black legend that "[w]ith porfirianism, the democratic, representative and federal state disappeared to be substituted for an absolutist, personalistic, and dictatorial power; liberties and the Rights of Man, dead on the page, were effective only for a reduced number of the dictator's friends."[5] The intellectual justification for this departure from a liberal constitution was supplied by a new positivist ideology, derived from the philosophy of the French thinker Auguste Comte (1798–1857) and not to be confused with legal positivism. Thus, it is the interruption of Mexico's constitutional tradition during the Porfiriato that has long been emphasized in most works on the subject.[6]

Although aspects of this narrative have certainly begun to be challenged, it continues to exert a strong influence over our thinking about the period.[7] To take up but one recent example, Howard Wiarda, evidently relying on an earlier history of Mexican liberalism, has argued that when Porfirio Díaz came to power in 1876 the "most recent of Mexico's occasional liberal episodes came to an end" and that "positivism supplied a programmatic roadmap for the [new] regime." Consequently, "liberal constitutionalism" was abandoned and "positivists" redefined constitutional "liberty" so as to make it practically meaningless. Although the regime paid lip service to such key concepts of nineteenth-century liberalism as liberty, their new meanings had "nothing to do with what North Americans would think of as individual civil and human rights."[8]

I begin with this particular historiography not only because it has emphasized the interruption of Mexico's constitutional tradition and therefore has tended to obscure important elements of Porfirian history but also because it cannot be reconciled with a peculiar paradox of the history of the Constituent Congress of 1916–1917, a point I will substantiate in a later chapter. As several revisionist scholars have argued, not only was ideological consensus within the Congress more significant than many traditional accounts would have us believe, it was a consensus profoundly shaped by constitutional developments and debates that took place *during the Porfiriato*.[9] In other words, the constitutionalism of the Constituent Congress did not hark back to liberal understandings common during the Restored Republic (1867–1876). This is especially clear with respect to amparo and the federal judicial power, although it is also evident with respect to the Constituent Congress's treatment of other key provisions, including the division of powers, especially a strengthened executive. If the Constitution was revered only in theory and ignored in practice, as Daniel Cosío Villegas asserted more than half a century ago, then how do we explain the very real constitutional changes that took place during this period and that seem to have informed so much of the work of the constitutional deputies who wrote the new Constitution of 1917? Any preliminary answer that engages seriously with the kinds of reforms made in 1916–1917 must admit that although some constitutional norms were ignored in practice during the Porfiriato, others were not. Constitutional practice put constitutional norms "in play" and often brought about, sometimes deliberately, sometimes not, constitutional change. Indeed, one of the principal tasks in what follows is to chart some of the most important constitutional changes as these relate to amparo and individual constitutional rights during this period.

Although it is tempting to test Bolaños's claim that the protection of constitutional liberties to property and person provided by amparo was a key factor in the making of the Pax Porfiriana, I will not treat the functional relation of amparo to political stability here. Bolaños's words may nonetheless be considered as a first piece of evidence in substantiating my argument in the first section of this chapter; its content is indeed illustrative of the high regard with which most jurists of this period regarded amparo. This section therefore argues that the suit's apotheosis (in the works of Bolaños and other jurists) must be understood at least in part as a Porfirian accomplishment. Because such a periodization, one that locates the apotheosis of a suit protecting individual constitutional rights in the middle of the Porfiriato, will strike many as odd or simply unlikely, a third section attempts to reconcile it with a more traditional understanding of Porfirian history. It does so by emphasizing how some of the most significant changes made in the constitutional interpretation of the suit and the suit's protection of individual constitutional rights appear to complement more than they contradict the predominant tendencies of the Porfirian state-building project between 1884 and 1910. These include the inadmissibility of the suit for settling political questions (especially those political questions that related to contested elections) and, perhaps less well known, the suit's increasing admissibility in settling property disputes and other questions relating to the application of the civil law of the states. Although some of my conclusions (especially with respect to the adjudication of property disputes) must be considered tentative, it seems unlikely that Díaz was able to directly control or manipulate these complex jurisprudential developments. Nonetheless, Díaz benefited from these developments in his quest to consolidate power in a strong centralized state. By glossing these two developments and prominent legists' and jurists' responses to them, I hope to make the day-to-day practice of amparo "thinkable" to those who are more familiar with the regime's acceptance of Comtean Positivism (privileging "order and material progress" over individual rights) than with its (simultaneous) affirmation of a constitutional jurisprudence protecting liberal individual rights.

A fourth and final section takes up the question of whether amparo and the constitutional rights that it most consistently protected were effective only in protecting members of the oligarchy or whether they had an application beyond the narrow strata of the political and economic elite. Again, these conclusions must be considered preliminary, but there is sufficient anecdotal evidence culled from judicial sources to suggest that amparo, although no elixir stone, was in fact used quite regularly by the nonelite as well as the elite. However, it must also be acknowledged that lack of access to the courts or knowledge of one's rights created insurmountable barriers for some. This fourth section may be thought of as a qualification of the argument of the third section that suggests a very close relationship between amparo and the very processes of modernization that favored the political and economic power of the Porfirian oligarchy under the guise of liberal constitutionalism. Amparo was thus simultaneously implicated in these processes and yet not simply reducible to them, which also helps explain why a strengthened and independent amparo court could be considered a Revolutionary reform by Conventionalists and Constitutionalists alike in the years after 1910.

Early Limits to Amparo and Its Porfirian Apotheosis

It was not until the return to a federal constitutional system in 1847 that the protection and enforceability of constitutional rights became an exclusively judicial process inspired not by European precedents (as in the creation in 1836 of a Poder Conservador, which can be traced to the ideas of the French liberal Benjamin Constant) but by the North American example of judicial review.[10] According to article 25 of the reforms to the 1824 Constitution (drafted by the well-known Mexican jurist Mariano Otero), "The federal tribunals will protect all inhabitants of the republic in the exercise and conservation of those rights that the Constitution and constitutional laws provide, against all violations by the legislative and executive powers, whether of the federation or of the states; said tribunals shall be confined to providing redress in the particular case to which the complaint refers and shall not make any general declarations with respect to the law or act that motivates it."

A similar provision was later to be incorporated into the Constitution of 1857. Article 101 specified that amparo was to proceed against any public authority that infringed one of the first twenty-nine articles of the Constitution (titled "Of the Rights of Man") or that represented an invasion of the jurisdiction of the states by the federation (or vice versa, an invasion of the jurisdiction of the federation by the states). Article 102 retained the original formulation of Mariano Otero, explaining that these controversies were always to take the form of a judicial suit and "[t]he sentence shall always be so drawn as to affect exclusively private individuals, and shall be confined to affording them redress in the special case to which the complaint refers, without making any general declarations with respect to the law or act that motivates it." According to the jurist Ignacio Vallarta, amparo was "the legal process intended to summarily recover any of the rights of man set forth in the Constitution and attacked by any authority of whatever category or to release them from the duty to comply with a law or command of an authority that has invaded the federal sphere or local sphere, respectively."[11] The rights protected by amparo included the now-classic bourgeois freedoms of speech, press, thought, life, industry, property, labor, and association. Amparo also protected the inviolability of domicile, papers, and possessions without just cause and the rights of the accused to a fair trial and defense and prohibited the creation of special courts, the use of torture, and the retroactive application of the law.

Although promulgated in 1857, these particular provisions did not find their way into practice until the passage of regulatory legislation in 1861. This legislation (the "organic law of amparo") was soon suspended in the face of the French Intervention (1862–1867), which in 1864 established a constitutional monarchy under the reign of the Austrian archduke Maximilian von Hapsburg. In 1868, following the 1867 reestablishment of republican government in Mexico City, new legislation was drafted that made amparo a suit of two instances, a first instance at the district level with a second, mandatory revision before the Supreme Court.[12] With this legislation, and with the elimination of the Court's handling of civil and criminal cases from the Federal District and federal territories on appeal, deciding amparos was to become the Supreme Court's most important jurisdictional function.[13] In short, the Supreme Court became an "amparo court" and the uninterrupted practice of amparo adjudication from 1867 until 1914 meant that by the twentieth century Mexico was one of the few countries in the world with an established legal tradition of the judicial defense of liberal constitutional rights.

Although institutions similar in kind to amparo have become a commonplace of twentieth-century constitutional law the world over, it must be remembered that in the last third of the nineteenth century this kind of institution was a substantial innovation and one that involved a significant break with an earlier paradigm. While amparo directly guaranteed a classic bundle of individual rights under the rubric of the "Rights of Man," it indirectly substituted a regime of constitutional adjudication for the supremacy of the popular legislature by making amparo a judicial process. This challenge to a key liberal value on the French model (i.e., the apotheosis of popular sovereignty) proved especially controversial among the framers of the Constitution of 1857. Indeed, it should not be forgotten that articles 101 and 102 of that constitution passed only after the insertion of a jury requirement, a substantial check on the creation of a strengthened judicial power charged with the control of constitutionality through the protection of liberal individual rights and the federal structure. That the jury provision was eliminated in the final version of the Constitution by the draft committee in consultation with the Committee of the Constitution reinforces the general impression that despite the strong precedent for these two articles in the 1847 reforms to the Constitution of 1824, the grafting of a system of "judicial supremacy" onto the Constitution of 1857 was the work of an "enlightened" minority within the Congress.[14]

Prior to the establishment of amparo in the Mexican constitutions of midcentury, the ideal of a limited government was to be realized principally through the active political participation of its citizenry (especially their use of the franchise), penal sanctions for authorities who overstepped their legally circumscribed spheres of action (*juicio de responsabilidad*), and in a federal republic, a division of power between the states and the federation. To see how this earlier paradigm of legislative supremacy and its corollary of a "sharp separation of legislative from judicial power" mitigated against the adoption of amparo, it is enough to quote the objections to the suit made by one of the best-known delegates to the Constituent Congress (later a Supreme Court justice), Ignacio Ramírez.[15] "What in reality they would like is for the tribunals to have, from now on, the capacity to partially nullify the laws and revoke the orders of all other authorities." When an authority violates the laws and the Constitution, then a case should be filed directly against this authority; this "is the path for making effective responsibility." However, in the "system invented by the committee" one power "repeals the laws" and another "makes them, which is contrary to every principle of jurisprudence."[16]

The right to choose one's government representatives lay at the heart of the liberalism that had emanated from the French Revolution, and it was an ideal that had guided Mexican republicans since at least the 1824 Constitution. Their liberalism therefore presented a serious obstacle to the creation of "a judicial power superior to the sovereignty of the people," as the delegate Anaya Hermosillo objected.[17] The emphasis within this earlier paradigm on majoritarian rule by virtuous citizens precluded, ipso facto, the supremacy of a magistracy of legal experts.

Yet as I have already suggested, amparo was implemented, and if its reconciliation with Mexico's liberal constitutional tradition was by no means inevitable, it nonetheless entered judicial practice, becoming the most important single factor in the creation of a Mexican body of constitutional jurisprudence, a jurisprudence that took as its principal point of reference the amparo decisions of the Supreme Court. There was a political barrier as well, and as late as 1882 the president of the Supreme Court, Ignacio Vallarta, could still harbor doubts about the perceived compatibility of the suit and Mexico's future political development that had little to nothing to do with Mexico's earlier liberal tradition.[18] With hindsight, Vallarta's doubts, preserved in the introduction to his magnum opus, *El juicio de amparo y el writ of habeas corpus* (The amparo suit and the writ of habeas corpus), appear to have been unfounded. Amparo would not only endure as constitutional practice throughout the Porfiriato, but during the twenty-year period from 1887 to 1907 the federal judicial power would resolve the unprecedented number of approximately fifty-seven thousand amparo suits.[19] It also seems likely that the efficacy of these decisions was drastically improved during this period, so that the lament of the secretary of justice in 1881 that problems around the enforceability of these judicial decisions were to be expected was to give way by the 1890s to the expectation that these decisions would be enforced regardless of the type of official responsible for the unconstitutional act.[20]

In a 1901 pamphlet, *Las conquistas trascendentales del derecho en México en el siglo XIX* (Transcendental conquests of law in Mexico in the nineteenth century), the jurist Antonio Ramos Pedrueza asked, "Has the recourse of amparo sufficiently penetrated our judicial habits? Has it responded to the real necessities of our political, social and economic life?" "[O]ur most notable jurisconsults," he observed, "have extolled the institution in such terms that it must be considered the most valuable achievement made . . . in Mexico in the field of our own judicial institutions."[21] By the time of the 1910 Revolution the suit's continued place as one of the most revered constitutional institutions was secure and it was continually praised as one of the truly great innovations of the Constitution of 1857; indeed, it was simply not subject to the criticisms leveled at other provisions of the Constitution as described by Daniel Cosío Villegas in his 1957 essay *La Constitución de 1857 y sus críticos* (The Constitution of 1857 and its critics). It is revealing along these lines that neither the Revolutionary Convention of Aguascalientes (1914–1915) nor the Constituent Congress of Querétaro (1916–1917) contemplated abolishing amparo, and even Emilio Rabasa, one of the most severe critics of the Constitution of 1857 according to Cosío, was to write in 1912 that the "Constituent Congress . . . reached on this point one or perhaps the greatest of its achievements to the applause of posterity."[22] For Félix Palavicini, one of the more forceful voices after 1913 favoring the drafting of a new constitution, amparo was one of two truly progressive and Revolutionary reforms that should be retained from the Constitution of 1857.[23]

Although there were certainly critics of the amparo suit, its consolidation and apotheosis as one of the central institutions of Mexican constitutional law clearly represent one of the most remarkable legal outcomes of Porfirian times. To the extent that this periodization is correct, however, it is not easily reconciled with the traditional image presented by the Revolutionary historiography of the Porfiriato. So now we must, insofar as it is possible, attempt such a reconciliation.

The Depoliticization of Amparo and the Court's Article 14 Jurisprudence

In what follows I will be charting some of the most important jurisprudential changes to the suit that also appear to have favored the larger trends and tendencies of the Porfirian regime. Such a focus should enable us to see why amparo could be consolidated during this particular period and why it enjoyed the full support of top officials of the federal government, including Díaz himself, despite the fact that amparo sometimes proved to be a check on the discretional use of state power. This synergy between jurisprudence and what we know from recent literature about the trends and tendencies of the regime is most clearly seen with respect to the Supreme Court's liberal jurisprudence around article 14, especially in regard to property rights as these were protected by the civil law, but it also had as one of its preconditions the depoliticization of the suit and the Court's refusal to protect political rights guaranteeing effective suffrage. With respect to both processes, the coming into being of a national rights regime during this period seems to have worked together with the political centralization for which the Porfiriato is so noted.

The depoliticization of amparo during the Porfiriato was a significant departure from practices and interpretations common during the Restored Republic. The central event in this process was the reversal of an interpretation of article 16 known as "incompetent by origin," used by the Supreme Court during the 1870s to intervene in electoral contests in the name of the political rights of the individual. According to article 16, "No one shall be molested in his person, family, domicile, papers or possessions, except by virtue of an order in writing of *the competent authority*, setting forth the legal cause upon which the measure is taken" (emphasis added). Simply stated, the doctrine of "incompetent by origin" said that any authority who arrived at his position or office by means other than those prescribed by law (for example, a free and fair election) was automatically incompetent to act in any capacity whatsoever. This jurisprudence, first formulated in 1871 but associated in most minds with the name of José María Iglesias, president of the Supreme Court from 1873 to 1876, was used to challenge the validity of several highly charged state-level elections during the Restored Republic, most notably in the Amparo Morelos of 1874. In his article "Constitutional Study on the Faculties of the Court of Justice," published in *El Foro*, Iglesias defended the Court's majority decision of April 11, 1874, that a Morelos state tax code of the previous year could not be enforced against the plaintiffs because the governor of Morelos who had signed the act into law was "illegitimate" and therefore "incompetent" to act in this capacity.[24] The governor was "incompetent by origin," as the phrase went, because his reelection to a second term, although declared legal by the properly constituted electoral college, had been in violation of the requirements of the state constitution.

The jurist credited with successfully overturning the doctrine of incompetent by origin is Ignacio Vallarta. Although the reasons Vallarta gave as president of the Supreme Court in 1878 centered on a defense of federalism, the larger context for the later acceptance of Vallarta's jurisprudence on this question was surely the events of 1876. Vallarta, a committed liberal delegate to the Constituent Congress of 1856–1857 and an important political player in his native state of Jalisco, was critical of the way this doctrine had been used by Iglesias as a weapon in the struggle over Sebastián Lerdo de Tejada's reelection to the presidency. Although a supporter of Díaz and the Tuxtepec cause and therefore a beneficiary of Iglesias's opposition to Lerdo, Vallarta moved to insulate the Supreme Court from the highly politicized contests for national and state power in which Iglesias had been a partisan.[25] Perhaps the most influential constitutional jurist of the early Porfirian period, Vallarta returned permanently to private life after 1882.

In 1883 the jurist Fernando Vega, glossing the new organic law of amparo of 1882, celebrated this new interpretation of article 16 that Vallarta had helped to establish. According to Vega, the use of amparo to contest elections or to assess the legitimacy or illegitimacy of an authority by any means, as Iglesias had done, was simply "unsustainable," and "it was condemned and cursed by the monstrosity of its own consequences."[26] The jurist Eduardo Ruíz also applauded the removal of amparo from its politicized use in electoral contests. In an 1888 treatise on administrative and constitutional law he described the Court's jurisprudence, arguing that the competency clause could be taken to mean only "constitutional competence," by which he meant a sphere of action determined by the constitutional division of powers and which he opposed to the "so-called competence of origin, which is nothing more than the legitimacy or illegitimacy of an appointment."[27]

The belief that the Court could not judge the "legitimacy of an appointment" as an indirect means of protecting political rights soon hardened into dogma, and we may presume that the famous Porfirian jurist Jacinto Pallares (a persistent critic of the Porfirian regime) did not believe he was saying anything especially inflammatory when, on the occasion of Vallarta's wake, he referred to those who had supported the "incompetent by origin" thesis as "irresponsible justices" willing to put at risk half a century of struggle for "democracy and the separation of powers."[28] Years later Emilio Rabasa was to criticize this jurisprudence in a similar vein and with the same assumption of consensus.[29] The belief that the Court was at its best when it calmly deliberated over a strictly juridical question and refused to decide "political questions," although far more complicated in practice than usually acknowledged, also reinforced a process already underway in which political rights would be separated out from "commonsense" understandings of natural rights.[30] As Miguel González Avelar has shown, this dogma was to go unchallenged by the Constituent Congress of 1916–1917 and endure for most of the twentieth century.[31] Amparo's later failure to adequately protect political rights would appear to be one of the principal legacies of the Vallarta Court.[32]

Although this development has recently been decried by scholars of Mexico's judicial power, it seems likely that it was a prerequisite for amparo's continued existence during the Porfiriato.[33] Formal elections would continue to be held throughout the Díaz era, but they came to serve a merely formal function, confirming results that had been determined beforehand by Díaz and his *camarilla*.[34] The Supreme Court, by removing itself from a confrontation with the machine politics of the era, would continue to operate as an amparo court now that it did not present a direct threat to Díaz's control of the political process. This control, however, also meant that Díaz was able to determine the individual membership of the Court, a fact that had important implications for judicial independence and the functioning of the Court's jurisdictional controls more generally. By law, the "election" of justices was to be "indirect in the first degree," each election following a six-year term.[35] In practice, one contemporary observed, "the justices of the Court are named by the executive."[36] Indeed, by his second four-year term if not before, Díaz controlled the selection of justices to the Supreme Court and the appointment of federal judgeships in the districts as well.

The career path of a Supreme Court justice during the Porfiriato, as the late François-Xavier Guerra has shown, was not unlike the career path of a federal deputy or senator.[37] Justice Miguel Bolaños Cacho, for example, began his political career as a local deputy in the state legislature of Chihuahua, became a federal deputy in 1896, was a justice on the Court from 1904 to 1906, and left that position to become a senator representing the state of Tamaulipas. With the outbreak of the Revolution he returned to his native Oaxaca, where he took over the governorship of that state during the Madero period.[38] Justice Carlos Flores was elected to the Chamber of Deputies multiple times before joining the Court in 1908, as was Demetrio Sodi, who also held several local judgeships and was the attorney general (*fiscal*) for the federal district of Colima prior to serving on the Court.[39] Although most justices remained on the Court for their full elected term of six years, less than half were reelected for multiple terms, and only a few enjoyed a tenure of more than twelve years.[40]

Despite executive control of appointments and the considerable flux in the Court's membership over the years, it is also likely that claims about the absolute subservience of the Supreme Court to the whims of the executive branch—by historians as well as contemporaries—have probably been overstated. Certainly some of the individuals who passed through the Court during these years were eager to please Díaz, and inevitably this was sometimes reflected in the way they decided certain cases.[41] However, decisions were by no means always unanimous, and many of the individuals appointed to the Court by Díaz were prominent liberal politicians and thinkers in their own right who probably exercised more autonomy in deciding amparo cases (at least in the realm of the "nonpolitical," as this had come to be defined) than has previously been recognized.[42]

To mention just a few of the more prominent individuals I have in mind: José María Lozano, author of numerous juridical works, including an important compilation of laws that still carries his name (along with that of his collaborator, Manuel Dublán), fought against the French, opposed Benito Juárez's reelection in 1870, supported Lerdo in 1871, and had been a member of the Supreme Court during the Revolution of Tuxtepec. He reentered public life in 1880 as attorney general of the Federal District and also operated a private practice until 1888. To cite one example of his relative autonomy from the regime, in 1885 he joined forces with several other lawyers to defend Enrique Chavarri, who was being charged with sedition for his strong attacks against the Díaz government in the pages of *El Monitor Republicano*.[43] Nonetheless, in 1888 he was appointed to the Supreme Court, a position he held until his death in 1893.

Manuel María de Zamacona, an especially influential justice on the Court from 1892 to 1904, had been secretary of foreign relations under Juárez in 1861, had been elected to the Chamber of Deputies on multiple occasions, and had been a prominent member of the liberal opposition to Juárez and Lerdo during the Restored Republic. Just prior to his appointment to the Court, he contemplated a run for the presidency against Díaz. Silvestre Moreno Cora, a true jurisconsult, was secretary general of government in his native state of Veracruz before he joined the Court in 1898. Though certainly more conservative than many of the other justices, especially in regard to church-state issues, his conduct as a justice was highly regarded and he authored one of the better-known books on the amparo suit, which he published in 1902. He left the Court in 1904, returning to the increasingly lucrative field of private practice.

Eustaquio Buelna, a native of Sinaloa, had joined the guerilla forces of Plácido Vega supporting the Plan of Ayutla, and later he fought against the French. He was prefect of Culiacán in 1855 and provisional governor of Sinaloa in 1856. In 1867–1868 he was a district judge in the state of Mexico before returning to Sinaloa to become a justice of the Superior Tribunal of Justice. In 1886 he joined the Supreme Court, where, according to Lucio Cabrera, he distinguished himself as an independent-minded justice willing to stand up to the secretary of development on questions relating to the surveying of public lands.[44] He remained on the Court for twenty years.

Demetrio Sodi, already mentioned, was also highly regarded as a jurist and an independent magistrate and was elected president of the Court on multiple occasions.

Certainly these short biographies, although only a partial sample of the total membership, do not fit the profile of a Court made up exclusively of Díaz's political cronies or a Court whose membership was uninterested in the liberal institutions that had emerged from the Reform era. The ideal of a liberal legal system made up of abstract general precepts that then could be applied on a case-by-case basis in a calculable fashion constrained the institutional life of the Court and meant that its actions followed a logic not solely reducible to the logic of the camarilla politics for which the Porfirian era is so well known. This is something to keep in mind as we turn to the history of the constitutional jurisprudence around article 14's changing constitutional interpretation.

As legal scholars have frequently remarked, the changing importance of what has come to be called "the cassation function of the Court" is largely the story of amparo's use in civil jurisdiction against the decisions of state-level judges, also known as the civil amparo (*amparo civil*). It is of interest here not only because it is one of the most significant judge-made expansions of federal judicial power during this period but also because its ultimate effect, the centralization of civil litigation, mirrors the political centralization exhibited elsewhere. The size and scale of this juridical transformation, following a trajectory largely determined by article 14's changing interpretation, is clearly discerned in the numbers. Although of little importance during the 1870s and 1880s, article 14 became, by the twentieth century, the most frequently applied article in constitutional adjudication outside of article 16, representing 2,292 out of 4,007 total suits in 1907.[45] The importance of article 14 turned on the reading of its second fraction, which read, "No person shall be tried or sentenced except under laws previously enacted, *exactly applicable to the case*, and by a tribunal previously established by law" (emphasis added). The question was, did this guarantee permit the federal judiciary to overturn the decisions of local tribunals if the civil law was not "exactly applied"? The Porfirian judiciary initially restricted the use of article 14 in this capacity but eventually answered yes to this question, resulting in an important and sweeping expansion of federal judicial power at the expense of the civil jurisdiction of the states.

This development, though interpreted by many Porfirian jurists at the time as the making of a more effective regime protecting liberal individual rights to property, also had consequences that have been criticized in the twentieth century, following, more often than not, the arguments first set forth by the well-known Porfirian jurist Emilio Rabasa. It must be noted that Rabasa was not an outsider to the Porfirian system. He had been a deputy to the state legislatures of Chiapas (1881) and Oaxaca (1883–1885) and a local judge and governor of Chiapas between 1891 and 1894. He then became a senator, first representing his home state of Chiapas and later Sinaloa. He was also influential as a jurist and professor of law. It is no surprise that his writings and commentaries about the Porfirian regime have carried historical weight.

Rabasa wrote two books that directly took up the question of amparo and its place in Mexican constitutional theory and practice. Both contain sustained polemics against this development but only the first, *El artículo 14*, published in 1906, is devoted exclusively to this particular expansion of the federal judicial power, initially as it related to the criminal jurisdiction of the states and then later in civil jurisdiction (the civil amparo). Rabasa argued that the way amparo was being used at the time was a violation of the local jurisdiction of these tribunals, leading to a de facto (and according to Rabasa, unconstitutional) centralization of the administration of justice; he also alleged that the use of amparo to overturn the decisions of state-level courts distorted the true function of amparo as a constitutional suit, flooding the Supreme Court with cases that were not truly constitutional in nature and, in the years immediately preceding the publication of his book, creating a backlog of crisis proportions. The solution Rabasa proposed was a constitutional amendment that would eliminate the second fraction of article 14 from the Constitution.

Before beginning my own survey of this development, however, some basic parameters need to be set by delineating four distinct periods or stages of changing interpretation: the first, from 1868 to 1879, comprises the early years of controversy over the organic law of 1869 that began with the indictment by the Chamber of Deputies of seven Supreme Court justices; the second period, from 1879 to 1888, is characterized by the influential jurisprudence of Ignacio Vallarta; a third stage, from 1888 to 1900, covers the triumph of the expansive or "liberal interpretation" with respect to article 14 (reversing the influential jurisprudence of Vallarta); and finally, a fourth period covers the backlog crisis (1900–1909), during which time the Court was unable to process in a timely manner its jurisdictional business. It was this crisis that prompted both Rabasa's 1906 book and the 1908 constitutional reform to article 102.

The first period begins in 1869 with the promulgation of a new organic law for amparo that transformed judicial practice. The new law's most important innovation has already been mentioned: the law made amparo a suit of two instances with a first instance at the district level and a second, mandatory, revision before the Supreme Court. The new law also barred the suit's use in "judicial matters." In this it clearly represented the institution of amparo as it might have looked under the 1847 reforms, which had restricted amparo's use to violations of the legislative and executive branches of government. However, under the 1857 Constitution this law clearly contradicted the wording of article 101 that amparo was to proceed against *all authorities* for constitutional violations of individual rights. The law also contradicted the Supreme Court's previous practice of admitting suits against judicial authorities. In its act of April 29, 1869, the Supreme Court continued this practice when it revoked the decision by the district court of Sinaloa to deny amparo to Miguel Vega against acts of the state's judicial authorities.

In response to the Supreme Court's nullification of a provision passed by Congress several months before (and supported by President Juárez), this same Congress moved on May 6 to indict those justices responsible for the majority decision, including León Guzmán, Ignacio Ramírez, José María Castillo Velasco, Simón Guzmán, Pedro Ordaz, Joaquin Cardoso, and Vicente Riva Palacio. However, as the jurist Blas José Gutiérrez recounted, "[D]espite the efforts of the accusers and the various wrongful summons sent to the accused by the Section of the Grand Jury . . . , on May 29, the summons were not obeyed, . . . the accusation being then reduced to a simple scandal without consequences."[46] According to Ignacio Vallarta, the resolution of this crisis in favor of the Court's position was also of special significance. "It resulted in the recognition of the fundamental principle of our institutions, which establishes that it is the faculty of the Supreme Court, as final interpreter of the Constitution, to declare in the specific case that it judges the unconstitutionality of a law even of the federal Congress."[47]

As Rabasa underscored as part of his own analysis, those suits that were filed and granted against local judicial decisions in the years after the Vega decision only occasionally took the form of a violation of article 14's guarantee of "the exact application" of the law.[48] Moreover, when the Supreme Court did decide an amparo for violation of article 14, it remained adamant that it could not and should not become a court of revision for local tribunals. With hindsight, it seems fair to conclude that the Supreme Court of the Restored Republic still exercised a significant degree of judicial restraint with regard to this question. As José María Lozano remarked at the time, "The majority of the Court has established that amparo only proceeds [for a violation of the second fraction of article 14] as a result of applying a legislation to a case that is not its own."[49]

However, Lozano also expressed doubts about the majority's interpretation of the second fraction of article 14.[50] He suggested in his 1876 treatise on constitutional rights that article 14 had been intended only as a guarantee in criminal jurisdiction and not for violations of the civil law. Among other reasons, Lozano suggested that the terms *judged* and *sentenced* did not apply to persons in civil litigation but only to those facing criminal charges, an argument impugned by Rabasa in *El artículo 14*. As Rabasa wrote years later, repeating in essence this earlier argument of 1906, "[I]t is enough to look at the article of the constitution of 43 that inspired this article in order to be convinced that the words 'to judge and to sentence' were then constitutionally applicable to both civil and criminal matters because it says that no one can be judged or sentenced in their *civil and criminal causes*."[51]

Nonetheless, this interpretation was to be adopted by Ignacio Vallarta as president of the first Porfirian court (1877–1882), and it eventually became the established jurisprudence of the Court following the Amparo Larrache (1879). This interpretation allowed for the Court's intervention in criminal matters for grievances involving "life and liberty" but not in the sphere of civil jurisdiction. For Vallarta, as for Lozano, the second fraction of article 14 had never been intended by the Constituent Congress of 1856–1857 as a right in civil disputes. Furthermore, to "exactly apply" the law in civil cases, argued Vallarta, was essentially devoid of meaning since judges were frequently asked to settle disputes for which there existed no previously established law. The same could not be said for a judge passing a criminal sentence.[52] In the words of the Larrache decision, "[I]f it is clear that the exact application of the law cannot be an individual guarantee when it comes to civil matters, by contrast in criminal matters it is," because "no criminal can be sentenced by analogy, *mayoría de razon*, etc., and that this principle is the one that the Constituent Congress wanted to sanction in article 14 of the Constitution."[53]

Vallarta's interpretation of article 14 was to endure as established jurisprudence for the next nine years—that is, almost as long as the jurisprudence that it overturned. In a decision of March 26, 1885, for example, the Court wrote, "[I]n repeated decisions, this Supreme Court has resolved that the exact application of the law required by constitutional article 14 refers to criminal cases and not civil ones." The reasons given in support were taken verbatim from the Larrache decision. Denying federal protection to Francisco Salinas, for example, the district judge of Zacatecas wrote, "[E]ven when the said authority, disobeying the laws of procedure, injures the rights of the complainant, this will not be an injury reparable through amparo because a multitude of sentences exist in which the Supreme Court declares that the abuses of judicial authorities and even personal outrages committed in a civil suit are not cases for amparo."[54] Many more examples could be given. For most of the 1880s, then, Vallarta, now in private practice, was able to advise those he represented as counsel that not only did he continue to oppose the thesis that amparo could proceed for violations of article 14 in civil cases, but the jurisprudence that he helped establish on this question was the uninterrupted practice of the Court.[55] Indeed, it was not until 1888 that the second fraction of article 14 was once again applied to the field of civil litigation in several important decisions.

Following this switch, and with the exception of a brief resurgence of a restrictive jurisprudence during the early 1890s, the Court used article 14 from the late 1880s on to regularly overturn decisions of local judges in both civil and criminal cases.[56] In the Amparo Zapata, for example, the Court intervened in a controversy over a last will and testament for violations of the state of Tabasco's law of civil procedure, granting amparo to the "legitimate" daughter doña Pomposa Dueñas de Zapata Vera, and this despite the fact that she had another action pending at the local level. In the words of the decision, "[T]he legitimate power that the aggrieved party to a judicial resolution has to appeal is not grounds for throwing out [*declarar improcedente*] an amparo because this suit is not subsidiary, nor extraordinary nor after another but a constitutional suit that proceeds anytime that there is a violation of guarantees."[57] That same day the Court also moved to publish Novoa's study of the case, a motion first proposed by Justice Zamacona, who congratulated the Court "for the final arrival of a jurisprudence" that resolved so many questions that until recently had continued to plague the Court. These included the matter of the admissibility of amparo prior to the final sentence in a civil suit and whether "what is called the judicial discretion [*arbitro judicial*] of ordinary judges is so inviolable that Federal Tribunals cannot apply their own criteria to the facts and their related principles." For both Novoa and Zamacona, the answer to this last question had to be no.[58]

This "liberal interpretation of article 14," as it was dubbed at the time, was recognized in the new regulatory legislation for amparo in 1897. The only restriction placed on amparo for inexact application of the law in this new legislation was that the violation had to be "notorious." However, as Miguel Mejía had already written a decade earlier, the liberal interpretation did not

> sustain the admissibility of amparo in all cases in which the exact application of the law is more or less debatable, but only in those in which the judge has pronounced a sentence notoriously unjust, either for having violated a clear disposition of the law, or by being manifestly contrary to that which is plain in the facts of the case, or for not being based in any law, or for basing itself in that which has no relation to the case, or for any other motives in which, more than a debatable interpretation of a vague or unclear law, there is true arbitrariness against which we have established the amparo.[59]

It is no exaggeration to say that the acceptance of this liberal interpretation by the Court was the most important change made with respect to the practice of amparo since 1869. In effect, the result of this jurisprudence was, as Rabasa argued in 1906, a de facto centralization of justice with respect to the adjudication of property disputes. Although there were other articles that could have accomplished a similar result in stabilizing and protecting property rights, article 14's specificity with respect to the judicial process and its openness with respect to what constituted an "exact application" of the law made it especially suitable for the task. In an annual address of 1907 the president of the Supreme Court concluded that violations against property resolved by the Court via amparo had been far more numerous than any other type.[60] Such an assertion would have been unimaginable to the Court of the 1880s, whose restrictive jurisprudence with respect to article 14 and the civil jurisdiction of the states had maintained that the vast majority of suits related to a question of property were to be resolved at the local level. Those legal professionals who were most committed to a closed and calculable system of civil law, unattainable without the intervention of the federal judicial power, strongly supported this development.

It is true that Vallarta's jurisprudence continued to be defended by important members of the Mexican legal profession even after the new interpretation became the established position of the Supreme Court. However, Rabasa's assertion that Vallarta's jurisprudence remained the dominant one held by Mexican lawyers throughout the period seems doubtful.[61] Jacinto Pallares, for one, predicted the triumph of the new interpretation from early on, explaining that Mexico's juridical tradition clearly supported it.[62] Prisciliano Díaz González, another well-respected member of the legal profession, argued for it on numerous occasions, as did other prominent jurists who remained committed to an understanding of the normative superiority of the rights protected by amparo because they were natural rights.[63] In the Court, an expansive jurisprudence found its principal champions in justices Manuel María Zamacona and Eduardo Novoa, and though Justo Sierra continued to insist on the old jurisprudence into the twentieth century, his behavior on the Court was somewhat of an anomaly.[64] Silvestre Moreno Cora remarked in 1902 that with respect to the suit's admissibility against the local judicial system for violations of article 14 there was complete consensus.[65]

It is this background that must be kept in mind if one is to understand the debates leading up to the 1908 constitutional reform to article 102. The question of the suit's admissibility in judicial matters was widely regarded as a settled question by the first years of the twentieth century. Rabasa, of course, was an important exception and he would play an important role in the push for reform. Although Rabasa's critique of article 14 probably remained a minority position, most parties to the debate came to agree that some kind of legislative reform was necessary as it became increasingly apparent that the federal judicial power could not keep up with an increasing backlog of cases. This backlog, beginning around 1900, reached the unprecedented level of 3,481 cases in the year June 1, 1905–May 31, 1906, and prevented the Court from deciding amparo cases in a timely manner.[66]

Some parties to the debate recommended reforms to the legislation of 1897. Others suggested constitutional reforms that would limit the use of the civil amparo but not completely eliminate it. Rabasa represented the most extreme position: a drastic reversal of the Court's liberal jurisprudence through legislative fiat. Although Rabasa's diagnosis of the problem has come to be accepted by most authors looking back on this period, many at the time took issue with Rabasa's argument that article 14 was the main cause for the backlog.[67] Moreover, few jurists saw the admissibility of amparo against judicial authorities as a simple revision or cassation of the decisions of the lower courts. Esteva Ruiz, writing under the pen name of "a moderate liberal," seems to have been much closer to the prevailing view of the time when he argued that the Supreme Court, when deciding a violation of article 14, was deciding a constitutional question (of individual guarantees) and not just applying the civil law.[68]

A series of proposals submitted to the Colegio de Abogados in 1906, which included Esteva Ruiz's, all suggested possible reforms to constitutional procedure intended to ease the labor of the Court. Although almost all of the essays recommended changes that would restrict the civil amparo to a certain extent, they were unanimous in keeping the admissibility of the suit against judicial authorities. One essay urged the treating of amparo in *salas*, or chambers, which would speed the work of the Court and would make any restriction unnecessary. Others still urged its restriction to a final resolution in a manner similar to the organic law of 1882. According to the winning essay, to not admit amparo against the errors of the local justice system for any reason was "illogical" if this meant "depriving a private person of their rights or imposing obligations which are not theirs in justice."[69] Even if the Supreme Court was not infallible, "while the administration of justice remains as distant as it is now from the ideal of a competent and perfect administration;

while its tribunals don't resist such frequent influencing, or for their ignorance, or for considerations having little to do with justice, there will continue to be a necessity that cannot be left unsatisfied without abandoning rights that should be protected, rights for which there exists a Supreme Tribunal for the whole country that, removed from mixed passions and little hates and free from the atmosphere of the provinces, judges by the light of an exclusively juridical criteria." The author, who was none other than Antonio Díaz Soto y Gama, warned against instituting hard and fast rules against admitting amparo. "It is not advisable to fix for the Court a priori the legal rules that prohibit the concession of amparo. . . . [W]hen they [the Court] encounter a case poorly resolved or poorly applied, only then should they judge when an error or an injustice by a judge constitutes a violation of rights."[70]

The constitutional reform to article 102 that came in 1908, however, did not reflect the suggestions of this prizewinning essay or of the spokesmen for the Colegio de Abogados. In prohibiting the use of amparo against judicial authorities for all but the final sentencing, the Federal Congress seemed to have recognized Rabasa's diagnosis of the problem as valid, although it did not go as far as he had hoped. As we are told by Bolaños, even the initial project of the reform was the outcome of considerable political compromise. Approved by the Chamber of Deputies, it then met significant opposition in the Senate.[71]

As the product of compromise on all sides, the reform, perhaps unsurprisingly, was widely criticized when it came time to assess its success or failure in practice. The Mexican Academy of Jurisprudence and Legislation lamented in 1910 that the changes made to article 102 were plagued with defects. Not only did the actual wording prohibiting the use of amparo against judicial acts prior to sentencing lack the necessary clarity, it left a significant number of serious violations of individual rights without recourse to the federal judiciary. This was, the academy underscored, contrary to the spirit and nature of the amparo suit. They also suggested that by taking into account only one aspect of the problem of "excessive use," the reform's ultimate effect had been to aggravate the present labor of the Court.[72] Although by 1910 the backlog had been eliminated, the president of the Court, Demetrio Sodi, explained that while the Court had done its best to follow the change mandated by the new constitutional reform, it had been necessary to "avoid the opposite pitfall of servility to the text, the undue and exaggerated restriction related to amparo's admissibility."[73] Venustiano Carranza would later conclude that it was essentially the Court's resistance to the reform's restriction on its powers to decide the "admissibility of amparo" in these cases that prevented the constitutional reform from operating the way it was intended.[74] Rabasa's criticisms of the reform followed shortly after, even though he had been a primary proponent of the reform and had even defended it in the debates in the Senate.[75] With the Revolution already in full swing, a legislative response to the problems with the 1908 constitutional reform would have to await the Constituent Congress of 1916–1917.

The Nonelite Presence in the Judicial Record

The point, then, is that, especially with respect to article 14, the kinds of jurisprudential changes I have been discussing had to operate within the institutional logic of a liberal court of law that played an undeniable role in structuring these particular outcomes. Nonetheless, it is striking that both the depoliticization of the suit and the Court's article 14 jurisprudence clearly favored the predominant tendencies of the regime. Also striking is the extent to which both of these developments enjoyed the support of one group in particular—the legal profession itself. As Alejandro Mayagoitia has pointed out for several of the same individuals I have been citing, these were not the lawyers (*letrados*) of the first half of the nineteenth century but instead were "true capitalist professionals," a new type of lawyer combining business and law along with their academic pursuits.[76] Although many of them also held government posts at different times, the fields of private practice and business were far more lucrative and the set of rights protected by amparo served to stabilize expectations, a functional requirement of the kind of capitalist economy that this group wanted to realize in Mexico. Following what is perhaps a somewhat simplistic class analysis, then, it should hardly surprise that a suit that guaranteed "bourgeois liberties" was defended and increasingly extended to include most property conflicts by this growing class of capitalist professionals.

However, the economic interests that legal professionals had in amparo (and these developments in particular) were not exclusively self-interested, and it would be a mistake to unmask a one-sided normative account of amparo with an equally one-sided interest-based account. Above all, it must be admitted that there was a certain excess to this liberal constitutional suit that did not always serve the interests of don Porfirio or a particular social class. The protection of rights that purported to be equally distributed and calculably adjudicated (at least at the level of theory) thus appears in Mexico, as elsewhere during the nineteenth century, as a double-edged sword that the political outs and the nonelite members of society were also able to make use of in opposition to elite impositions, especially with regard to acts at the local level, against which most amparo suits were filed. In what follows, then, I want to mention three areas in which the amparo decisions of the federal judicial power seem to indicate that such an "excess" did in fact exist in the day-to-day practice of rights adjudication. These include examples relating to the "land question," forced recruitment into the military, and arbitrary imprisonment.

The historian Robert Knowlton has addressed the first of these areas with reference to the implementation of the laws of disentailment, a central theme of Revolutionary historiography.[77] Knowlton's main claim is that despite the long history of legislation stipulating and regulating the breakup of pueblo or indigenous communal landholdings into small (private) family plots, the judicial record reveals that even into the twentieth century conflicts around disentailment and communal property were still being decided by the federal courts.[78] In other words, this central piece of Reform-era liberal legislation was by no means consummated prior to the Revolution, indicating (perhaps) a larger margin for successful resistance to such liberal state projects imposed from above than has sometimes been assumed. The judicial record that Knowlton has in mind is the published decisions of the federal judicial power to be found in *El Semanario Judicial de la Federación*, and he begins with the influential Porfirian jurisprudence established by Ignacio Vallarta.

Knowlton suggests that even though Ignacio Vallarta famously denied that Indian communities could litigate as "moral persons" in 1882 (Amparo Remigio Bautista), individual members of village communities were able to make use of the amparo suit during this period to block the breakup of communal property.[79] This fact, he argues, challenges the idea that nonelite groups were powerless against the wealth and caprice of the Porfirian elite. Knowlton's findings, then, are an important corrective to some of the more extreme views that have been put forward in the historiography about the subordination of the Porfirian judiciary to the class interests of an oligarchy.[80]

A significant number of the cases cited by Knowlton concern article 16. In 1888, for example, one Francisco Olivares was extended federal protection on the basis of article 16 by the Supreme Court against acts of the municipal president of San Bartolo Teontepec, Puebla. According to the facts of the case, the municipal president claimed he was simply implementing the disentailment laws, specifically the Circular of December 20, 1856. However, as the Court noted, simply by moving against a piece of land that was currently in the possession of Olivares as heir and executor of the will of José María Solis, this executive official had dispossessed Olivares of the property in question without a hearing or defense before a court of law. Therefore, the municipal president had decided a contentious issue involving the rights of the complainant, and since "only the judicial power has competence, following the appropriate legal procedures, for addressing contentious questions," the municipal president was in clear violation of article 16.[81] The decision of the Supreme Court, delivered on February 17, 1888, declared null and void the actions taken by the municipal president and restored Francisco Olivares to possession of the lands in question.

The basic doctrine of constitutional competency on which this decision was based was by no means novel, nor was it restricted to conflicts over communal and individual property. Moreover, it was an interpretation that was effective not only against the unconstitutional acts of municipal authorities but also against those of state governors. In another case cited by Knowlton, various residents of Huimanguillo, Tabasco, filed amparo against the acts of the governor of the state who had ordered the division (*deslinde y fraccionamiento*) of village properties. The complainants who demonstrated through proofs that they had been in possession of this land alleged violations of their constitutionally protected rights, citing articles 14, 16, 17, and 27. The grant of federal protection in their favor concluded, "[T]he complainants are in possession of lands and houses of which they have been deprived without being heard or defeated in a civil suit before the competent authority; and since this dispossession was executed by an administrative order verifying the division of the same lands that were sold to other persons without the proper legal formalities, so the procedure lacks a *motive and legal cause to justify it.*"[82]

In 1904 the Supreme Court decided another case in favor of the village of Calimaya. Several months earlier the governor of the state of Mexico had signed a contract with one Luis Díaz de la Vega for the exploitation of certain woodlands that originally belonged to the village. Although the governor had received permission from the municipal government before concluding the contract, he was nonetheless opposed by the complainants, who were currently using that land and who argued in their brief that neither the municipal authorities nor the governor had the right to make such an agreement. Initially the district judge disagreed, siding with the state authorities and noting that the lands in question had in fact been managed over the past few years by the municipal government, which charged fees for its use.

However, the Supreme Court overturned this decision, saying that the complainants had proven that "the lands of Calimaya are owned by the community for the use and benefit of the residents of the population."[83] If the laws of disentailment in question recognized the ownership of these lands by the community, the Court reasoned, then by concluding a rental contract without their consent, the governor had attacked article 16 of the Constitution. This decision was in complete agreement with jurisprudence established in 1882 by Ignacio Vallarta in the Amparo Cirpriano Castillo Mercado, the first case that Knowlton cites.

Amparo was also successfully used to oppose the *leva*, the method of forced recruitment into the military. According to Moises González Navarro, "the leva was the normal manner of integrating the army and only the poor succumbed to it."[84] However, from 1877 to 1910 the Supreme Court aggressively opposed this practice, ruling that outside of voluntary recruitment and the lottery, forced conscription was a violation of constitutional rights. In 1887, for example, approximately 880 soldiers successfully filed suit against their forced conscription into the military and were set free on the basis of these Supreme Court decisions.[85] However, it is clear that amparo also had its limits, for despite this opposition by the Court, the practice of the leva seems to have continued into the twentieth century and was not truly abolished until after the Mexican Revolution.

The Court also resolved amparo cases that involved illegal or arbitrary imprisonment. On February 18, 1890, for example, one Plácido Ramírez was detained for begging and later consigned to the Hospital of the Poor in the city of Guadalajara, where he was indefinitely held against his will. Against his detention and naming the *jefe político*, or political chief, of Guadalajara as the responsible authority, Ramírez filed amparo. He claimed that he had not been begging the day of his initial detention but buying a shirt, and three witnesses testified to his status as a working man able to secure "the basic necessities of life," and this "despite the [unspecified] ills which inflict him." The district judge ruled granting amparo against the reclaimed acts, a decision that was confirmed by the Supreme Court one week later.[86]

In another case that was filed against the acts of a different political chief, León Vázquez asked for amparo from his cell in Pénjamo, Guanajuato. He maintained that he had been detained for several months (in fact, only thirty-six days) and feared that he might be deported. By the time the district judge had received his request, Vázquez had indeed been deported, but only to the nearby district of Piedad. The judge immediately decreed the suspension of the act but he then stayed the suit itself, presumably because Vázquez had been set free by the authorities. On August 23, 1905, the Supreme Court revoked this decision by the district judge, deciding definitively in favor of Vázquez in a unanimous decision citing violations of article 16 (*molestias sin fundamento*). The Court also ordered the consignment of the political chief of Pénjamo to the appropriate judicial authorities, charging him with criminal conduct in an application of article 823 of the Federal Code of Civil Procedure.[87]

In September 1906 amparo was also granted to Juan Flores in response to a petition filed by Benito Flores in Juan's name. The original detention had been ordered by the justice of the peace (*juez de paz*) of Acatlan Chiconquiaco, Veracruz, for the killing of a turkey, property of one Gandelaria Garcia. However, in the absence of any written justification for these acts, the district judge felt compelled to nullify the order of detention, setting Juan Flores free, a decision that was then confirmed by the Supreme Court in a unanimous decision.[88]

If these examples allow us to imagine how prominent revolutionaries (especially those who were legal professionals) could still be committed to amparo as a Revolutionary institution in the years after 1910, it must also be remembered that there are certainly other examples in which amparo failed to do justice or correct for the many abuses of governmental power that have been documented elsewhere. However, if the consensus within the legal profession and among large segments of the elite around the importance of the amparo suit as the keystone of a Mexican theory of limited government was fragile at best during the 1860s, it was a consensus consolidated by the twentieth century—a fact we would be hard-pressed to explain without reference to the continual practice of constitutional defense by the federal judicial power during the Porfiriato. It was a consensus that the framers of the Revolutionary Constitution of 1917 were never to call into question, a difference that clearly distinguished their work from the liberals of 1857.

CHAPTER TWO

From the Plan of San Luis Potosi to the Constitution of 1917

> [I]t was necessary to make the social revolution within the governmental mechanism and not to occupy the land or the house or support the worker, the campesino or the employee by the force of arms, but by that more permanent and stable force: that of the laws.
>
> —Félix Palavicini, 1930

> [T]he Mexican Revolution will have the legitimate pride of demonstrating to the world that it is the first to incorporate into a constitution the sacred rights of the workers.
>
> —Alfonso Cravioto, 1916

Early histories of the Mexican Revolution distinguished at least two periods within a single revolutionary process. The first period was the revolution led by Francisco Madero in 1910 but confined to the principles of effective suffrage, no reelection, and other liberal political rights. This revolution was successful to the extent that it deposed Porfirio Díaz and brought Madero to power in November 1911 through a free and fair election, the first truly competitive presidential election in recent memory. Fifteen months later, however, Madero was deposed in turn by a counterrevolution led by several distinguished generals from the old Porfirian army. One of these generals, Victoriano Huerta, became the new president. The second period was the revolution led by Venustiano Carranza against the Huerta government in 1913. According to this earlier historiography, this second period culminated in the drafting of a new constitution. Although this second revolution inherited the mantle of the first (along with its aspirations for political democracy and the successful implementation of liberal constitutionalism), it addressed socioeconomic grievances directly through constitutional reform. The new constitution, it was said, represented the institutionalization of popular Revolutionary claims for social justice, specifically the passage of "protective legislation for workers and campesinos."[1]

As historians have emphasized, the original formulation of social legislation by the pro-Carranza faction after 1914 was not bestowed on the masses by the leadership of a victorious revolution. Quite the contrary. Social legislation like the agrarian law of January 6, 1915, was promulgated at a moment of profound weakness, civil war, and uncertainty. This has sometimes been obscured by earlier histories of the Revolution that emphasized the socioeconomic reforms of the Constitution of 1917 as the telos of a single Revolutionary struggle. It therefore makes sense to begin with a brief political history of the Revolution itself in order to better understand the process by which socioeconomic grievances—largely absent from Madero's 1910 call to revolution—became constitutional law.

Francisco Madero was born into a well-to-do family in the northern state of Coahuila in 1873. He was educated in Mexico, the United States, and Paris and became a successful *hacendado.* In other words, he was a prominent member of the Porfirian elite. In 1904–1905 he launched an unsuccessful bid for the governorship of Coahuila, and in 1910, following Díaz's public declaration that he would not seek reelection (a declaration that was subsequently retracted), he made an unsuccessful bid for president of the republic. Madero was an unlikely challenger for the presidency but his surprising surge in popularity in 1910—enhanced no doubt by the self-imposed temporary exile to Europe of another potential challenger, Gen. Bernardo Reyes—nonetheless forced the Porfirian regime into open persecution of Madero's Anti-reelectionist Party. Indeed, just prior to the June elections, Madero and many of his supporters were imprisoned in a bare-knuckled display of arbitrary power. On October 5, 1910, following his release on bail, Madero fled across the border to the United States. There he conferred with other oppositionist leaders in San Antonio, Texas, and drafted his Plan of San Luis Potosi, decrying the electoral fraud of June and July and calling for the violent overthrow of the established government in Mexico City.[2] His call to revolution, according to the historian Paul Garner, "was a classic nineteenth-century *pronunciamiento*," not unlike Díaz's own plan to overthrow the government of thirty-four years earlier.[3] Madero denounced the illegality of the presidential election, called for the people to take up arms, and promised new elections once his revolution was victorious.

Initially Madero's revolution appeared to go nowhere; the time and date Madero had set for the uprising (6:00 p.m., November 20, 1910) came and went with Díaz as firmly entrenched in power as ever. Secret preparations for the revolt inside the country were uncovered and suppressed, most spectacularly in Puebla but also in other urban centers, including Guadalajara, Chihuahua, and Hermosillo. Men and women known for their sympathies toward Madero's antireelectionist cause were imprisoned and Madero, having crossed back into Mexico on November 18, 1910, with plans to attack the town of Piedras Negras, was forced to return to Texas when the expected number of promised supporters failed to materialize.[4]

Nonetheless, some insurrectionary movements did take place on November 20, most successfully in the northern state of Chihuahua. The inability of federal forces to definitively crush these rebels and the numerous other revolts that soon were taking place in the states of Durango, Sonora, and Sinaloa inspired other anti-Díaz groups to take up arms, and by April of the following year a revolution of national proportions had put the government forces on the defensive. Madero reentered the country in February 1911 and assumed the leadership of the most important Revolutionary forces in the north. With the successful capture of Ciudad Juárez on May 9, 1911, the government finally conceded to rebel demands and Díaz was ousted from power.

It is important to keep in mind that the Plan of San Luis Potosi barely mentioned the social problems that in hindsight appear so central to the history of the Mexican Revolution. The plan focused almost exclusively on the illegality and electoral fraud of the 1910 elections and it understandably sought support from as many discontented parties as possible. Indeed, it was successful in achieving a cross-class alliance that may have otherwise been fragmented by references to a redistributive social program of the sort articulated by the Mexican Liberal Party Plan of 1906 with which it is so often contrasted. But for one important exception to be explored below, the Plan of San Luis Potosi was devoid of a program to address the kind of socioeconomic grievances that were to play such an important role in the consolidation of a new order after 1917.[5]

Revolutionary grievances for social justice did not, however, emerge sui generis in the period after 1913. The conditions that provided the grounds for their later formulation were present throughout most of the Porfiriato. Prior to 1910, however, their articulation by so-called precursors of the Revolution—the anarchist radicals of the PLM (Partido Liberal Mexicano), workers, rural community leaders, or adherents to the cause of social Catholicism—were marginalized through repression by an effective and coercive state apparatus.

Although carried out in the name of political, not social, reform, the Madero revolution nonetheless undermined to a significant degree this coercive apparatus.[6] It was during this first crucial period of revolutionary insurrection, then, that workers were emboldened to organize and press their grievances and that the radical agrarian program of Emiliano Zapata was first formulated. Indeed, it was during the period 1911–1913 that the government tolerated strikes and organizing drives for the first time in Mexican history, leading to an important increase in union membership.[7] Anarchists and other radicals, persecuted for their publications prior to 1910, benefited from the lifting of restrictions on the press and free speech. A new government bureaucracy, the Department of Labor, was established by interim president Francisco León de la Barra to deal with mounting industrial conflict and it recognized (to a certain extent) the legitimacy of workers' grievances. This new government bureaucracy was instrumental in negotiating the first industry-wide minimum-wage scale in the textile industry.[8] Work was also begun on a proposal for a unified labor code.[9]

The Madero revolution also emboldened the leaders of rural communities, dirt farmers or campesinos, and "peones," rural workers on large landed estates, although the extent to which this political action was then translated into concrete benefits during these early years is not as clear as in the case of industrial labor. Here Emiliano Zapata's early break with Madero due to his gradualist approach to the land question is often considered the canonical example. Nonetheless, it was the Plan of Ayala, announcing Zapata's break with Madero on November 25, 1911, that would later inspire some of the most radical reforms of the Revolutionary era.[10] The plan proclaimed continued commitment to the original Plan of San Luis Potosi, specifically its second provision, which also promised the return of all lands to the "numerous small land-holders, the majority of them indigenous peoples, [who] have been dispossessed of their lands." It withdrew recognition of Madero for turning his back on this Revolutionary promise and offered leadership of the new revolution to Pascual Orozco (hero and leader of the battle for Ciudad Juárez) or, if he refused to accept, Emiliano Zapata. Article 7 of the Plan of Ayala decreed that, "in virtue of the fact that the immense majority of Mexican pueblos and citizens are owners of no more than the land they walk on, suffering the horrors of poverty without being able to improve their social condition in any way or to dedicate themselves to industry or agriculture, because lands, timber, and water are monopolized in a few hands, for this cause there will be expropriated the third part of those monopolies from the powerful proprietors, with prior indemnification." Those who opposed the plan, either "directly or indirectly," however, could expect to have their property nationalized with no indemnity.

Although Zapatismo, as this movement for land redistribution became known, pushed for the radicalization of the Revolution, other insurrectionary movements against Madero sought a restoration of the old Porfirian order. These included two short-lived revolts against the government in 1911 and 1912 by two important Porfirian generals. The first revolt, which took place in September 1911, was led by Gen. Bernardo Reyes. The second revolt, which began thirteen months later, was led by Gen. Félix Díaz, nephew of don Porfirio. Both were quickly put down and both generals were imprisoned.

Both generals continued to conspire against the new government, however, and in February 1913 they launched a third revolt from their prison cells in Mexico City with the aid of Gen. Manuel Mondragón and the covert support of U.S. ambassador Henry Lane Wilson. After eight days of fighting, during which Bernardo Reyes, among many others, was killed, Madero was taken captive by his own forces. A fifth collaborator in the conspiracy, Gen. Victoriano Huerta, assumed the position of provisional president. Four days later Madero and vice president José María Pino Suarez were taken from their prison cells and murdered, probably on Huerta's orders.[11]

With General Huerta in power, the new privileges being exercised by organized labor, though not immediately revoked, were eventually curtailed, and within the year the anarcho-syndicalist organization COM (Casa del Obrero Mundial) was banned and many of its leaders were jailed. Political liberties were attacked, press freedoms were suspended, and on several occasions Huerta appears to have ordered the murder of those who opposed him.[12] This reign of political terror was not confined to the capital (indeed, the Maderista governor of the far northern state of Chihuahua, Abraham González, was one of its first victims), but it was in the capital that its consequences were most vividly and, for polite society, most shockingly played out. To mention one of the best-known examples, in September 1913 Deputy Belisario Domínguez was murdered because of a speech he delivered in the Chamber of Deputies that included a call for impeachment proceedings against Huerta, an incident that forced Congress into an open conflict with the executive. Huerta responded by dissolving Congress (using as his pretext a very different conflict between Congress and the Supreme Court) and jailing those whose loyalty to him was suspect.

If these kinds of actions helped discredit Huerta among the very classes that originally welcomed his leadership, not to mention the interested eyes of the international community, it was outside the capital that a new and even more powerful insurrectionary movement was gathering strength in opposition to Huerta's coup and his counter-Revolutionary policies. As with the Revolution of 1910, this new revolution emerged strongest in the north, but with a new leader: the governor of Coahuila, Venustiano Carranza.[13] On March 4 Carranza announced his refusal to recognize the legitimacy of Huerta's provisional government. He was the only governor to do so. Twenty-two days later, from his ranch in Coahuila, Carranza issued his Plan of Guadalupe, calling for a second revolution.

The plan was short and legalistic, even more so than Madero's Plan of San Luis Potosi. It began by accusing Huerta of treason. In support, the plan cited a message "sent to the state governors communicating to them that [Huerta] had imprisoned the Supreme Magistrates of the Nation and their Cabinet." "Whereas," the plan continued, "the Legislative and Judicial Powers, despite the laws and constitutional rules to the contrary, have recognized and protected General Victoriano Huerta and his illegal and unpatriotic procedures . . . [we] the undersigned, Chiefs and Officers commanding the constitutional forces, have agreed and will sustain with arms the following [plan]." The plan itself was divided into seven articles. The first refused to recognize General Huerta as president of the republic. The second withdrew recognition of the legislative and judicial branches. The third gave those state governments that had recognized Huerta thirty days to withdraw their recognition. The fourth named Venustiano Carranza head of the Revolutionary army. The fifth specified that the "first chief" (Carranza) would become provisional president upon the occupation of Mexico City. The sixth provided for national elections after the triumph of the Revolution and the seventh and final article, for the reconstitution of the powers of the states.

This second revolution was largely unsuccessful in Carranza's home state of Coahuila. On three separate occasions in 1913 Carranza's forces were defeated by Huerta's.[14] In the adjoining state of Chihuahua and the state of Sonora, however, insurrectionary movements met with more success. In Chihuahua, what began as multiple and disparate guerrilla movements against superior federal forces eventually transformed itself into a large and formidable conventional army under the command of Gen. Pancho Villa. On October 1, 1913, Villa took the key strategic city of Torreón, Coahuila. He then turned back to the north to consolidate his control of Chihuahua, taking Ciudad Juárez a few weeks later.[15] By the end of the year Villa controlled most of the state. Another major figure of this second revolution, Alvaro Obregón, led a separate Revolutionary army in the west. After consolidating his control in Sonora, Obregón marched south into Sinaloa, taking Culiacán by the end of November.[16] He then continued south through Nayarit and Jalisco, eventually taking Jalisco's capital city, Guadalajara, by the summer of 1914.

In the south, Emiliano Zapata benefited from this turn of events. Although he refused to endorse the Plan of Guadalupe, Zapata's forces continued their fight against the government after Huerta deposed Madero. Zapata's Liberating Army of the South was now able to mount an offensive that encompassed the states of Morelos, Guerrero, Puebla, Tlaxcala, and by midsummer 1914 they had advanced posts on the edge of Mexico City.[17] On June 23, 1914, Pancho Villa took the heavily garrisoned city of Zacatecas in one of the most important battles of the Revolution. With the federal army unable to contain or defeat rebel forces in either the north or the south, Huerta fled the country and on August 14, 1914, the interim president surrendered unconditionally to the northern revolutionaries.

The victorious Constitutionalists, as the northern revolutionaries called themselves, dissolved the federal army and closed all federal offices until new elections could be called. However, a smooth transition to a new Revolutionary government required compromises that the various emerging factions (already in evidence prior to their August victory) were unable to make, and a definitive split between the Revolutionary forces of Villa (the largest and most powerful of the Revolutionary armies, now in alliance with Zapata's Liberating Army of the South) and those of the civilian first chief, Venustiano Carranza, quickly devolved into an internal battle and civil war. The Revolutionary Convention of Aguascalientes, made up exclusively of military men, one representative for each one thousand soldiers, according to the Pact of Torreon, declared itself sovereign, appointed an interim president, accepted Zapata's Plan of Ayala, and appointed Pancho Villa the head of its armed forces. Carranza, having rejected the sovereign authority of the Convention of Aguascalientes, retreated to Veracruz, where he was joined by several of the generals who remained independent or third parties to the conflict between Carranza and Villa, including General Obregón.

The Supreme Court and the Madero Revolution

One of the striking continuities linking the Porfiriato with the Madero revolution was the continuity of federal judgeships.[18] This continuity appears in hindsight to have been an error in Madero's revolutionary strategy. One factor that must be taken into account if we are to understand this error is Francisco Carvajal's role as the chief government negotiator at the Treaties of Ciudad Juárez. Carvajal was a Supreme Court justice, elected to the Court in 1908. According to Lucio Cabrera, he was a confidant of both Díaz and Díaz's well-known (and controversial) treasury minister, José Yves Limantour. It seems likely that Carvajal's role in the treaty negotiations contributed to the continuity of judicial personnel. However, Madero's hands-off approach when it came to the judicial power probably had other sources as well. His initial inclination to respect the autonomy of the Porfirian Supreme Court and the absence of any attempt later to impose partisan candidates in order to create a "Maderista Court" followed logically from his strong commitment to liberal democratic principles and respect for the division of powers as established by the Constitution of 1857. The consequence of this, however, was that Madero inherited a Supreme Court that consistently, and under Carvajal's leadership especially, identified with the deposed Porfirian regime, a tendency that plagued Madero's political allies even after his murder in 1913.

Indeed, in the first year of Madero's presidency the justices of the Supreme Court elected Carvajal, one of the most "notorious partisans" of the old order, as chief justice.[19] Although a partial renovation of the Court took place later that fall (electing David Gutiérrez Allende, Jesús L. González, and Francisco Díaz Lombardo), this hardly tipped the scales decisively in Madero's favor. Just weeks prior to Madero's violent overthrow in February 1913, Jesús Novelo sent a secret memorandum to the president urging vigilance and concluding, among other things, that "all or almost all of the functionaries of the judicial power are enemies of the present government."[20]

Lucio Cabrera, the only scholar who has plumbed this period of Supreme Court history in any depth, singles out at least four important moments of political activity along these lines. First there was the Supreme Court's intervention in the military proceedings against Gen. Félix Díaz. Prior to his involvement in the successful coup of February 1913, Díaz had led a failed revolt against Madero in October 1912. Within a week, however, both General Díaz and his collaborators had been imprisoned, and soon after his capture Díaz was sentenced to death by a military tribunal (*consejo de guerra*). Against this sentence, Díaz filed amparo. He also petitioned the Supreme Court directly, asking them to intervene in the case pending at the district level. The Court, under Carvajal's leadership, reacted immediately, telegraphing both the military tribunal and the district judge of Veracruz, urging the latter to act before the sentence was carried out. In this way the Court weighed in on the side of Díaz, earning praise from conservatives and condemnation from the sector of public opinion sympathetic to Madero's revolution. The Supreme Court never heard the case. General Díaz's life was spared by a presidential pardon, but the Court's early intervention in this case even if it was not decisive was interpreted at the time as an openly political act favoring a Porfirian general hostile to the new regime.[21] The Court was also responsible for the transfer of Félix Díaz from a Veracruz prison to Mexico City, where he participated in the successful coup of February 1913.

The second moment relates to Victoriano Huerta's appointment to the presidency on February 18, 1913. On that day Huerta informed the Court of his new position at the head of the executive branch.[22] The next day the Court replied that it would continue to administer justice, implying that it would not intervene politically in the present conflict. Three days later the Court sent a formal letter of congratulations to Huerta. The letter was the work of three stalwarts of the old regime: Alonso Rodríguez Miramón, Emilio Bullé Goyri, and Carlos Flores, all of whom paid Huerta their respects later that afternoon.[23] Several months later Rodríguez Miramón and Bullé Goyri, along with Emilio Alvarez, Gutiérrez Allende, and González, would also contribute to a conflict with the Chamber of Deputies over grand jury proceedings filed against former minister of the treasury Limantour. This conflict in turn would provide partial grounds for Huerta to dissolve the Chamber of Deputies in October 1913.[24]

Finally, when Huerta did dissolve the Chamber of Deputies, imprisoning eighty-four deputies in the process, the Court abstained from extending judicial protection to those who had been illegally and unconstitutionally jailed. Although this would have been the appropriate and legal response, clearly in line with past precedent and the Court's jurisdictional function, the outcome would have been politically charged. It appears that the Court lacked the courage to confront Huerta over this particular issue, even indirectly. As Lucio Cabrera tells us, the Court busied itself with other matters instead of acting decisively in favor of those political prisoners held in arbitrary imprisonment.[25] With the victory of the Constitutionalist revolution in August 1914, the Supreme Court was closed. It would not reopen until June 1, 1917, and the new revolutionaries would work to ensure that the new Court was made up of individuals sympathetic to the Revolution and not the old order.[26]

Victory of the Constitutionalists and the New Additions to the Plan of Guadalupe

The original Plan of Guadalupe issued by Venustiano Carranza had made no mention of social reforms, although these were apparently discussed by some of the revolutionaries present at its signing, including a young captain who was later to play an important role in the drafting of a new constitution, Francisco Múgica. In late 1914, with the largest segments of the Revolutionary forces marching against him (and doing so under the banner of one of the most radical plans of agrarian reform that the Revolution had produced), Carranza proposed several important amendments to the Plan of Guadalupe, including concrete provisions for land and labor reforms. In his decree of December 16, 1914, issued from the port city of Veracruz, Carranza accused his enemies—most notably Pancho Villa—of being counter-Revolutionary and reactionary. Carranza reiterated his position as supreme chief of the Constitutionalist forces and his adherence to the Plan of Guadalupe. In a crucial amendment to the plan, however, Carranza added that he would now also be responsible for "drafting and putting into effect during the struggle all the laws, dispositions and measures designed to give satisfaction to *the economic, social and political needs of the country.*"[27] His list included references to agrarian laws that would "favor the small property" and "dissolve the *latifundia,*" labor laws that would "better the condition of the rural peon, the worker, the miner," and electoral laws that would guarantee "effective suffrage." On January 6, 1915, Carranza decreed a "pre-constitutional" agrarian law and in Veracruz several labor decrees, including minimum-wage protections, were implemented. These progressive labor policies enabled Carranza's top general, Obregón, to swell his ranks with new recruits from the urban working classes. Although probably not decisive for Obregón's later victories over Villa's forces in the battles of Celaya and León, these "Red battalions" of working-class recruits did shore up the numerically weaker forces under Obregón's command.

This new idea that political and social reforms could not wait for the reestablishment of constitutional rule as initially set out in the Plan of Guadalupe was not, as Frank Tannenbaum recognized long ago, "the proclamation by a victorious revolutionary army ready to establish a government for the purpose of bringing these reforms to pass. It was bait for attracting adherents to the cause, a means of justifying the independent existence of an army."[28] These social reforms were to have an important impact on the path Constitutionalism was to take in the months and years after the defeat of the Conventionalist forces led by Pancho Villa and Emiliano Zapata. As Adolfo Gilly writes, Carranza's "break with [Villa] . . . produced a radicalization of Constitutionalism, the function of which was to provide a social counterweight" to Villismo and Zapatismo.[29] Thus, a return to the unreformed Constitution of 1857 as originally promised by the Plan of Guadalupe was no longer possible. Indeed, on September 19, 1916, Venustiano Carranza convoked elections for delegates to a national assembly that would gather in Querétaro that December to rewrite the Constitution of 1857 and "raise to constitutional precepts the reforms dictated during the struggle."[30]

The Constituent Congress in Querétaro

It is, of course, the new socioeconomic rights to be found in articles 27 and 123 that most clearly bear the mark of the experiments in preconstitutional Revolutionary social reform. These new rights have quite frequently been singled out by historians of the Revolution, allowing the making of a new constitution to be represented as a culminating moment of Revolutionary transformation. Frank Tannenbaum writes of the Constituent Congress of 1916–1917 that it was probably "the most important single event in the history of the Revolution," and although some revisionist historians have taken issue with this claim, few have been willing to deny the radical nature of articles 27 and 123 in particular.[31] Article 27, which still belonged to the Constitution's first chapter, now titled "Of Individual Guarantees," reserved the right to alter the "modalities of private property" and included hydrocarbons in a list of mineral resources owned by the nation. It also established an agrarian reform making all agrarian communities eligible for "restitution" or "*dotación*," which in both cases involved the expropriation of privately owned agricultural properties.[32] Article 123, which became part of a new chapter, "Of Work and Social Security," created a set of far-reaching protections for workers and their families, including a priori employer liability with respect to work accidents; limits on maximum hours and a minimum wage; a mandated day of rest; a proposed system of labor arbitration boards to deal with capital-labor conflicts; required profit sharing; and the recognition of unions, collective bargaining, and the right to strike.

It therefore has been something of a caveat that despite the radical nature of these provisions (and a few other "social articles" related to church and state, education, etc.) the new document, taken as a whole and organized around principles of popular sovereignty, the division of powers, and individual constitutional rights, remained, to a large degree, within the classic nineteenth-century mold of a liberal constitution. To the extent that this paradox has been resolved by the traditional political historiography of the Revolution, it has been done with reference to a contentious political battle between two factions within the Constituent Congress, one classically liberal, civilian, and Carrancista, the other Jacobin, militant and Obregonista. The disjuncture between the original draft presented by Venustiano Carranza, a "merely political document" containing none of the radical social reforms of articles 27 and 123, and the final "social constitution" as hashed out after two months of debate, supplied the ultimate proof for this interpretation and was assumed also to be evidence of a larger political conflict taking place between the two Revolutionary caudillos.[33] The grafting of radical social provisions onto the trunk of what remained a liberal constitution was thus framed as the hard-won victory of the latter group over the "classical-liberal" stalwarts of Carrancismo, which nonetheless determined the Constitution's overall structure.[34]

The revisionism of the past forty years has largely displaced this narrative of two factions, emphasizing instead the significant degree of political and ideological autonomy exercised by the delegates.[35] It has been pointed out that General Obregón's role was not as decisive as it was originally assumed and that the polemical categories of "rightists" and "leftists," to be found in a handful of key debates, make for a poor set of analytical categories (either as civilian/military or liberal/"Jacobin") for understanding the making of a new constitution as a whole.[36] On the vast majority of articles, the voting patterns of the delegates do not follow these divisions and it has been shown that the conservative or "classical-liberal" faction was not as ideologically opposed to the new social rights as has sometimes been supposed. As Charles Cumberland has written, "When Palavicini [a so-called rightist], for example, suggested that the details of Article 27 would be more properly a matter of congressional act, he voiced a perfectly legitimate concern over the respective provinces of constitutional and statutory law; but nothing in his career could be interpreted as indicative of a rejection of agrarian reform. José Natividad Macías, considered by many as the very epitome of conservatism, helped draft both Articles 123 and 27 in their preliminary form. Pedro Chapa, another of the 'conservatives,' also signed both drafts, as did Samuel de los Santos."[37] Cumberland's emphasis on convergence over divergence in the ideological makeup of the Congress has been closely followed by Jorge Sayeg Helú and Bertha Ulloa in their more recent accounts and also explains how such a project was even possible given the considerable time restraints that were placed on the delegates.[38]

The debates relating to the judicial power are a case in point, as they are especially notable for the absence of two factions or parties divided along ideological lines; indeed, they are notable for ideological consensus on the big questions, though this certainly did not preclude, as was also the case with the socioeconomic reforms, acrimonious debate on the particular form certain changes to Carranza's proposals were to take. However, as José Ramón Cossío has recognized (and unlike the changes related to the socioeconomic reforms), none of the changes to the judicial power to be found in articles 94, 96, 98, 101, 105, and 107 modified "the liberal model nor the broad outlines of the constitutional model proposed by Carranza." Cossío's conclusion:

> If we analyze together the debates on the federal judiciary and the Supreme Court, we can say that the basic ideas revolved around first, that the duty of these bodies was to guarantee respect for individual rights through the amparo suit, that the exercise of this function was the best guarantee against dictatorship and despotism, that the federal system could only survive if this Power was strong, that its members should be honest and reputable, that the federal executive should not have a role in the appointment of judges and justices, and that members of the Court (at least the original one) should pass through a trial period.... The basic idea that guided its design was fundamentally liberal.[39]

Indeed, in agreeing on the general principles behind Carranza's proposal to strengthen judicial autonomy and supremacy, the delegates in fact displayed far more consensus than did the Constituent Congress of

1856–1857, a consequence of amparo's nineteenth-century evolution.[40] This consensus bridged the Revolutionary/anti-Revolutionary divide and Félix Palavicini, among many others, listed amparo as one of the truly great and Revolutionary innovations of the Constitution of 1857.[41] Besides consensus over the desirability of retaining the suit, however, the practice and experience of an amparo court after 1861 also provided an important framework within which those constitutional delegates familiar with the amparo law thought and talked about constitutional rights and the judicial power more generally. It is the ways in which this framework also determined the understanding of Revolutionary social reform and its relationship to the rest of the Constitution that will be my main concern here.

To summarize the most important reforms made to the judicial power, the Congress voted to change the size of the Court to eleven justices, approved a change to the quorum requirements, established lifetime tenure for Supreme Court justices (albeit after two trial periods, the first ending in 1919 and the second in 1923), and also modified the appointment process by adopting a system similar to the one used in the appointment of Mexico's very first Supreme Court in 1824, that is, election by the Congress acting in its function as an electoral college with the list of candidates submitted by the state legislatures.[42] This last reform, which modified article 96 of Carranza's original project, followed one of the more acrimonious debates relating to the judicial power. In particular, article 96 of the project met considerable resistance from a group of delegates including José María Truchuelo, Alberto M. González, Rafael Martínez Escobar, and Pastrana Jaimes, two of whom were later elected to the first Revolutionary Supreme Court in 1917. The reform to which they all objected provided that the justices were to be appointed by Congress in consultation with the executive, who was given the option of proposing additional candidates. While some defended the system of 1857, which provided for indirect "popular" election of justices without the intervention of the executive, other delegates agreed with the Second Committee on the Constitution that in practice this system had proven ineffective.

What is significant for our purposes in glossing this particular debate is not what could have been if congressional forces had been aligned differently but rather that despite these strong differences of opinion in the details, all parties to the debate seemed to agree that the controversy revolved around the best means to the commonly agreed upon end—a strengthened and reinvigorated judicial power and consequently an effective system of individual constitutional rights, or "individual guarantees." Moreover, in this and other debates it is striking the extent to which the delegates who participated (many of them from the so-called Jacobin wing of the Congress) were familiar with some of the most important debates of amparo jurisprudence. These included the question of the "incompetent by origin" doctrine, the question of whether the Supreme Court should be able to intervene against procedures and decisions of the local judiciary, and in the debate over article 96, the question of the political character of the judicial power itself.[43]

Rafael Martínez de Escobar's particular intervention in the debate over article 96 is an example of this point, although it differs from other interventions in its specific proposals. In attacking the proposed reforms that would have given the executive a role in the appointment process, Martínez de Escobar declared both lifetime tenure and popular election of justices as unrealistic for Mexico. He proposed instead that justices be appointed by the Senate or the Chamber of Deputies but "never, absolutely never, should we allow the executive power to be the one who has a direct or indirect intervention in the appointment of the justices of the Supreme Court of Justice."[44] He considered the judicial power a power on par with the other three powers of government. Its importance, he went on to explain, resides in its power "to fix the limits of the authority held by the other powers" and to tell the other branches of government "your powers go to here," and no more.[45] Martínez de Escobar's argument about the political character of the judicial power presupposed a particular theory of the division of powers and drew on a tradition of a long line of treatise and pamphlet writers on amparo, including (to name only the most famous) Lozano, Montiel y Duarte, Moreno, Vallarta, and Rabasa (mentioned by name as part of Martínez de Escobar's discourse), all of whom had weighed in on this particular question.

However, the following drew on this same tradition of liberal jurisprudence: "In this way, then, as the judicial power comes to define what is precisely the extension of right [and] what is the extension of the law; it has the mission of defining the limits of individual liberty and social liberty; when there is an invasion of social liberty by the individual and vice versa, as well as fixing the extension of the sovereignties that coexist in the Federation."[46] This opposition between the social and the individual as limit and right in this particular passage had already been emphasized by Martínez de Escobar in earlier debates and in a manner that was consistent with amparo's nineteenth-century evolution—an evolution that had made individual constitutional rights enforceable as part of a jurisdictional process (amparo) but had also made the notion of social limits imposed by law a commonplace of constitutional jurisprudence.

This brings us to an important if often overlooked point about the constitutionalization of Revolutionary social reform. Here, too, amparo jurisprudence and the constitutional categories that had emerged from a living tradition of constitutional-rights defense were to exert an important structuring force on the way that social reforms were to be incorporated into the Constitution and, most importantly for our purposes, the way Revolutionary-era social reforms were to be articulated as a set of new constitutional limits ("social rights") on individual rights. It is true, as one scholar has written, that "[i]n the discussions on articles 27 and 123, amparo hardly came up."[47] But in less obvious ways involving the received categories of constitutional law, amparo—and everything it presupposed—had a major impact on these particular debates. Indeed, one of these received categories critical for understanding the constitutionalization of Revolutionary social reform was the concept of social right itself. Of course, the concept itself has been something of a moving target, especially in the twentieth century. It was not, however, a concept invented by the revolutionaries and in a certain sense it was not even that revolutionary a concept. Indeed, if one were to survey its pre-Revolutionary use, one would come across the not-so-very-revolutionary Jorge Vera Estañol—a conservative lawyer and Huerta collaborator who felt that the Constitution of 1917 smacked of Bolshevism.[48] He used the concept in his classes on commercial law taught at the national school of jurisprudence prior to the Revolution. The concept of "social right," Vera Estañol explained to a class in 1908, "consists in the set of provisions that determine human freedom in its relation with society."[49]

To the claim that *social right* understood in this general sense was not Revolutionary, one must hasten to add that a defense of a concept of individual right, as seen in the Constituent Congress, should not be considered anti-Revolutionary. Yet the idea that those who defended individual rights in the Congress were also by definition conservatives (opposed to social reforms) has often been utilized in accounts that are looking to sustain the concept of two ideologically opposed factions. In one of the earliest and best-received treatments of the politics of the Constituent Congress, E. V. Niemeyer Jr. writes, "Herein lies the basic difference between the moderate rightists (or classical liberals) of the convention and the leftists: whereas the former placed the rights of the individual before those of society, the latter placed the rights of society before those of the individual. The rightists considered the chapter on individual rights as the most sacred part of the constitution; the leftists believed it necessary to modify these rights in the interests of society."[50] Given what I have already said about two factions and the unanimous support for amparo by all parties to the debate, there are already good reasons to doubt this account. But even in the limited debates where the politics of two factions is said to have broken out into the open, ideological conflict of the sort identified by Niemeyer seems rather less obvious when read in the light of the received categories of constitutional law and amparo jurisprudence (as opposed to the meaning these categories were going to take on later).

Already as part of the discussion on article 1, an older sense of a social right was to exert a certain degree of influence on the thinking of the delegates. The first chapter of the Constitution, explained Rafael Martínez de Escobar, the first person to invoke the category of social rights, is characterized by two kinds of rights: individual rights (*las garantías individuales*) and social rights (*las garantías sociales*). "In those articles we see in each thought a palpable liberty; in some, entire ones, we see a complete limitation on the individual in favor of society. . . . [I]n this way, the constitutional right is an individual right, [and] it is a social right."[51] As Andrés Lira González has written, "For Martínez de Escobar, the rights of man had been 'the great achievement, the monumental achievement,' but it was not only the rights of the individual but the rights of the individual in society that were established and, as such, it covered the rights of the individual and the rights of society."[52] Or as another member of the leftist wing of the Congress also noted, "[T]he law can limit these individual rights in certain cases." The idea, he suggested, was no different than that contained in the Constitution of 1857, interpreted, that is, by the Supreme Court and nineteenth-century jurists.[53] José Natividad Macías argued that social rights, belonging as they do "to the whole," could not be protected by the amparo suit because of their collective nature.[54]

In reflecting on the debate over article 3's right to education, perhaps one of the most contentious debates of the entire Congress, similar ideas were expressed by the "rightist" delegate Frederico Ibarra. "It is sufficient to carefully read the Constitution [of 1857] to see what has already been said here, that, in the chapter on individual guarantees, the Rights of Man that are to be constitutional guarantees are determined; these rights are determined first, defining a principle more or less general and then come their corresponding limitations, because there is no such thing as absolute liberties" *in a Constitution.*[55] This quotation, then, shares a similar set of conceptual oppositions with those made by the leftists who opposed Ibarra on this particular vote.[56] But the framework within which constitutional rights could be proposed and limited (and therefore also adjudicated before the Supreme Court) was the same.

In brief, the delegates were not divided between those who affirmed the importance of a charter of individual rights in the Constitution and those who did not. Those who have attempted to define the issue at stake in these terms have unsurprisingly found inconsistencies and contradictions in the behavior of some of the most important individual delegates in the debates that followed.[57] Rather, the language of higher rights that favored the individual was freely used by all parties to the debates that centered on the form and extent of the social limits to be placed on rights. When pressed, those opposing additional limits nonetheless had to admit that in principle such rights *could be* limited. That is, social rights existed in the Constitution of 1857 and would also exist in the new document. Even Ibarra, who is considered in the literature as one of the conservatives of the Congress, did not hesitate to assert in the same passage already cited above that there was no such thing as "absolute liberties" *in* the Constitution, a commonplace of amparo treatises that nonetheless frequently regarded individual rights in the Constitution to be derived from natural rights. However, these same "conservative" delegates also had recourse to an idiom of absolute liberties or natural rights that even the "Jacobin" or "leftist" Committee of the Constitution was openly willing to acknowledge. For example, the first Committee on the Constitution (to which Múgica belonged) called the right to think freely a natural right and held that, though it should be limited in society, it had its origins in a faculty born with the individual.[58]

The new social provisions introduced into article 27's right to property must also be seen in relation to this larger consensus, and though the new limits that were introduced were even more radical than those approved in article 3, they do not represent an exception to the general argument presented thus far. In other words, radical social reforms were proposed and conceptualized as necessary new limits on an individual right at the same time that that right (in this case property) was to be recognized in the Constitution. The Committee on the Constitution, in presenting its reformed version of article 27 (an earlier version had mentioned an agrarian reform but was rejected by the delegates as insufficiently specified), reiterated the importance of keeping the right to property as an individual guarantee yet it also underscored that this right was not and could not be considered "absolute." It had certain restrictions placed on it in the past and it would continue to have restrictions placed on it in the future. "As a consequence of the expressed, the Committee, after consecrating property as an individual right, protecting it from any expropriation that is not grounded in public utility, has fixed the restrictions to which this right is subject."[59] A constitutionally mandated agrarian reform was then included as a new limit on the constitutional right to property. It passed with ease following a unanimous vote on the last night of deliberations.

To argue that the place of protective legislation in favor of workers also stayed within this older conceptual framework of individual and social rights, however, is considerably less straightforward. The initial proposal to include new limits on article 5's freedom to work (this proposal included protections for women and children, a minimum wage, the eight-hour workday, and the six-day work week) was rejected by the Congress and these particular restrictions were then removed from title 1, chapter 1, and placed in their own chapter, titled "Of Work and Social Security," becoming article 123. To the extent that the proposals contained in article 123 (including additional proposals by many of the delegates, such as a priori employer liability for work accidents, profit sharing, the right to strike, etc.) did not seem to "fit" in the first chapter of the Constitution, it follows that a traditional notion of social right as social limit was similarly deemed inadequate. To what extent, then, was the conceptual framework that related social right to individual right within a liberal constitution transformed by the debates leading up to the final draft copy of article 123?

The objections to the eight-hour workday and other constitutional limits to be included in article 5 were of two kinds. There was a minority who argued that these kinds of limits did not belong in article 5 and that it was enough to specify, as Carranza's draft had, that labor legislation was to be drafted by the federal legislature. There were also the concerns of a majority who objected to the new reform by arguing that the small list of provisions included by the Committee of the Constitution was not enough. Those who defended the new limits on the freedom to work did so by emphasizing that restrictions on constitutional rights when in the interest of the public good were (as had been repeatedly voiced in the context of other debates) nothing new.

Despite its eloquent defense by such radicals as Francisco Múgica and Heriberto Jara (who even suggested that the social provisions could also be thought of as guarantees in favor of individual liberty in their own right), the reform was not going to pass as originally proposed.[60] The stalemate was broken when Deputy Froylán C. Manjarrez suggested the removal of the proposed legislation in favor of giving labor its own chapter and, furthermore, recommending that provisions be expanded to address the specific objections of those who had argued that the article did not go far enough. This motion easily passed (uniting the alleged antithetical ideological commitments of all those opposed) and Deputy Alfonso Cravioto affirmed the creation of a new article with his oft-quoted comparison with the French Revolution: "In the same way as France after their revolution had the high honor of consecrating in the first of their *Carta Magnas* the immortal Rights of Man, likewise, the Mexican Revolution will have the legitimate pride of demonstrating to the world that it is the first to incorporate into a constitution the sacred rights of the workers."[61]

Several historians have suggested that such statements indicate the creation of a new kind of subjective right, a clear departure from an understanding of social rights as limits placed on the rights of the individual. That this seems to have taken place with respect to the labor provisions but not with respect to the agrarian law has also led some to exclude article 27 from the tally of social rights in the new constitution.[62] Lucio Cabrera has gone so far as to suggest that the delegate Martínez de Escobar, quoted above, wanted amparo extended to protect social rights (conceived of as new individual rights favoring the economically disenfranchised) as well as traditional liberal individual rights but that this proposal was defeated in the course of debate on article 1.[63]

Although Alfonso Cravioto was clearly not the only one to suggest that social legislation in favor of workers was a matter of fundamental individual right and not just a new limit on an older set of constitutional rights (Múgica similarly suggested it was a matter of "natural right"), there are good reasons to believe that a transformation in the idea of what constituted a social right was not as complete or as far-reaching as has sometimes been implied.[64] There is little evidence, for example, that Martínez de Escobar's suggestion to change the title of the first chapter from "Of Individual Guarantees" to "Of Constitutional Guarantees" indicated a desire to have amparo proceed for infractions of article 123, that is, for the new constitutional rights of workers. Indeed, the silence with respect to the new labor provisions when the debates turned to the framing of a new judicial power makes clear that the inclusion of social legislation in favor of rural and urban workers had not yet prompted a fundamental rethinking of a traditional distinction within Mexico's constitutional tradition.

On the one hand, then, it seems likely that a break with liberal assumptions about society, the state, and the individual were not as far-reaching in the Constituent Congress of 1916–1917 as some retrospective accounts have implied. Such a break would happen soon enough, but this break is part of the history of the Constitution's implementation, not its framing. On the other hand, one corollary of this argument is that amparo helps explain why it was no accident, as V. B. Mirkine-Guetzévitch once implied, that Mexico's revolutionaries raised labor and agrarian reforms promised during the struggle to the level of constitutional law, making Mexico the very first among Latin American and European countries to constitutionalize labor and agrarian law.[65] To the extent that the vast majority of delegates to the Congress agreed on the need for labor and agrarian reforms, it makes sense that this kind of innovation would take place for the first time in a country that had a tradition of constitutional-rights adjudication, all the more so when the constitutional rights that were most commonly adjudicated related to classic "bourgeois" rights to security, liberty, and property and might be used to oppose the new social reforms. No European countries had this kind of tradition.

The formulation of Mexico's social rights was nonetheless understood at the time within a categorical framework peculiar to Mexico's constitutional experience. As originally conceived, then, Mexico's new social rights remained something of a prisoner to this older framework, first initiated as social limits on the Constitution's enumerated individual rights and not eligible to become rights actionable through the amparo suit. It was, of course, amparo that had ensured that a traditional bundle of liberal rights (raised to constitutional law in 1857) was not regarded as a set of "promises without sanction," as in most constitutions.[66]

In sum, the treatment of the judicial power and individual rights by the Constituent Congress allows us to conclude that if Martínez de Escobar had in fact contemplated the extension of amparo to include the new social rights, whether they be protections for workers, agrarian reform, or even the question of education, this certainly would have required a rethinking of amparo's function from a protection of purely negative rights to one that could command positive state action. As we have seen, this rethinking was clearly absent in his understanding of the judicial power in particular and in the general view expressed by the rest of the delegates. Rather, the strengthening of the judicial power was conceptualized as the principal defense of individual liberties against abuse by the public power. Although individual liberties were circumscribed by new social limits, the socioeconomic reforms of 1917 remained within a larger constitutional arrangement going back to 1857 and premised on a liberal vision of state and society.

Thus, if a refashioning of the idea of social right (something that clearly did take place later) was beginning to happen, it did not lead to a rethinking of amparo, nor did it invert or otherwise change the conceptual relation between fundamental individual rights and their necessary social limits, as understood in Mexico's constitutional jurisprudence. The line between the two remained the prerogative of the judiciary to decide. Individual rights were praised and defended by the most radical members of the Congress and they were intended to be implemented through a judicial process. The new social provisions, on the other hand, were to be realized through an administrative process, a fact that further reinforces the impression that social rights remained, for a majority, a question of constitutional limits as this concept had been understood prior to the Revolution. The executive branch took on new faculties (implementing the agrarian and labor provisions) but these new faculties would remain within the purview of judicial control as traditionally understood.

Although the reforms made to the Constitution of 1857 did not transform the categorical framework within which individual rights were conceived within the constitutional system as a whole, they did radically transform the content of some of those rights. This was especially true of the right to property, which, to paraphrase an American dictum against "class legislation," allowed the new Revolutionary state to take from A and give to B on the basis of need, although always respecting the "small property." Oil and other mineral resources could not be owned by those in possession of the topsoil, water resources that had previously been privately owned and managed were now "considered of public utility," and the private property of the shop floor was opened up to public intervention and labor legislation.[67] These modifications to the Constitution of 1857 did not render constitutional law or its interpretation meaningless, yet this is how many of the opponents of the new Revolutionary state portrayed it; they have been followed in this interpretation, curiously enough, by more recent "Marxist" interpretations of this constitutional transformation.[68]

Other rights previously contained in the first chapter of the Constitution of 1857, however, stayed essentially the same, and this was especially true for those rights most frequently adjudicated during the Porfiriato. Reforms to article 16 were blocked on two separate occasions by the Congress and it essentially reverted to the Constitution's 1857 wording in order to appease concerns that its future efficacy in favor of the individual and against arbitrary government acts would be as successful after the Revolution as it had been in the past. Article 14, however, did undergo significant reforms. It now read,

> No law shall be given retroactive effect to the prejudice of any person whatsoever.
>
> No person shall be deprived of life, liberty, property, possessions or rights without due process of law instituted before a duly created court in which the essential elements of procedure are observed and in accordance with previously existing laws.
>
> In criminal cases no penalty shall be imposed by mere analogy or even by a priori evidence, but the penalty shall be decreed by a law in every respect applicable to the crime in question.
>
> In civil suits the final judgment shall be according to the letter or the juridical interpretation of the law; in the absence of the latter, the general legal principles shall govern.

With hindsight we know that both of these articles played an important role in delaying the implementation of Revolutionary social reform despite its constitutionalization.

Does the foregoing amount to another argument alleging that bourgeois conservatism triumphed at Querétaro? This is certainly the kind of critique that some delegates would later level against themselves with the benefit of hindsight.[69] What I want to suggest by way of a conclusion is that in January 1917 it was still possible for even the radicals within the Constitutionalist revolution to imagine a "transformative" (and "revolutionary") politics that could bring about far-reaching social reforms in favor of workers and campesinos and yet also appropriate aspects of "bourgeois," or liberal, legality as this had been elaborated by Mexico's liberal jurists. With implementation, however, much of what had been retained may be viewed as naïve or shortsighted, but one must also keep in mind that the constitutionalization of agrarian and labor law carried out in Querétaro was the first of its kind.

The Bolshevik, Weimar, Austrian, and Czechoslovakian Constitutions would all come later. Moreover, unlike in the well-known case of the Weimar Constitution, the much-debated failures of which contributed to the rise of National Socialism (Nazism), the Mexican delegates to the Constituent Congress of 1916–1917 felt that they had a clear idea of how the new social norms would be articulated with the old (and necessary) liberal individual rights. Mexico's new constitution was not susceptible to the charge—to be articulated in Germany during the 1920s—that it had been a "decisionless constitution," simply juxtaposing the new and the old without any categorical framework to guide their proper relations.[70]

Thus, in adding the new social rights to the Constitution, most of the delegates to the Constituent Congress thought they had solved one of the most basic problems obstructing the realization of liberalism's promise of equality (and a principal cause of the Revolution), a solution that, nonetheless, can be said to have remained within the conceptual horizons of a nineteenth-century form of liberal-republican government (including judicial supremacy) and that reinforced key precepts of liberal constitutionalism inherited from the past. It must be recognized, then, that these new provisions were passed in the guise of new social limits on traditional liberal individual rights, a fact that, as the next two chapters describe, was to have important consequences for the adjudication of constitutional conflicts. Indeed, it will help to explain how it was even possible that a Supreme Court committed to the Revolution and appointed by delegates who had had a hand in incorporating Revolutionary social reforms into the Constitution could nonetheless decide constitutional cases against their implementation. Although it was Mexico's amparo suit that probably made the constitutionalization of redistributive social policy appear to be such a necessary and even self-evident reform to the delegates to the Constituent Congress, it was also this tradition that enabled those who opposed labor and agrarian reforms to successfully resist implementation by filing suit before a district judge and ultimately before the Supreme Court.

CHAPTER THREE

Liberal Jurisprudence and Article 123

> [A]rticle 123 has been scandalously violated; in effect it is not in force, we all know it; it is the Supreme Court of Justice, to a significant degree, who is at fault since they have made the labor boards completely useless.
>
> —Antonio Díaz Soto y Gama, 1921

As a matter of public law, the Revolution came to an end on May 1, 1917. The new president, former first chief of the Revolution Venustiano Carranza, was sworn into office on this date (national elections had taken place in March) and the new constitution, promulgated in February, went into effect. This is where those histories that have focused on the constitutionalization of Revolutionary social reform also end. However, as revisionist historians of the Mexican Revolution have frequently noted, raising these Revolutionary norms to the level of constitutional law was one thing, putting them into practice was another matter altogether.

The obstacle to implementation most frequently cited by historians was the need to pass regulatory legislation before these new constitutional norms could be put into effect. With respect to the new labor provisions this had to take place at the local or state level (per article 123) and this was done quickly in some states and not at all in others. However, those states with strong labor backing, which were able to move quickly, regulating and implementing some of the more radical principles of article 123, soon ran into an obstacle of another kind, namely, the resistance of the courts and of the Supreme Court in particular. How should this resistance be characterized?

Two very different interpretations immediately suggest themselves on the basis of the extant scholarship. The first, based on work written predominantly by political and social historians of the Revolution, tends to deny agency to the Supreme Court altogether, explaining these jurisprudential shifts in terms of changes in executive policy and assuming judicial subservience to the will of the executive. Thus an executive branch hostile to Revolutionary social reform best explains Supreme Court resistance to the implementation of radical state labor laws. A second interpretation, based on the work of legal scholars (trained in Mexican law) and generally ignored by historians of the Revolution, argues the opposite, that the Court's interpretation of state-level labor laws indicates instead the relative autonomy of the Supreme Court from executive interference. It makes sense to take this latter interpretation more seriously than historians have generally done. However, in the case of labor the datum of Supreme Court opposition is not as obvious an index of judicial autonomy as some scholars have assumed.

To be fair, the legal scholarship does not focus on the Revolutionary period exclusively. It has generally taken a much longer (and more general) view of these processes of institutional change, beginning in the 1860s when Mexico's Supreme Court began to make use of its powers of amparo. For example, Héctor Fix-Zamudio lists "differences of opinion between the federal executive and the Supreme Court from 1918–1929" related to Revolutionary social reform as just one of several important conflicts that might lead us to qualify the assumption of an uninterrupted judicial subservience to the executive. He also notes the conflict that occurred in the early years of the Restored Republic over article 8 of the organic law of 1869, barring amparo from overturning local judicial decisions, as well as the conflict that arose over the doctrine of "incompetent by origin" (see chapter 1) that pitted the Court against Lerdo's administration and helped bring Porfirio Díaz to power in 1876.[1]

The first Supreme Court to function under Díaz's tenure as president reversed this controversial jurisprudence, a move that, along with the removal of the chief justice from the presidential succession in 1882 (via a constitutional amendment), effectively depoliticized the Supreme Court. If this was a precondition for amparo's subsequent consolidation, as already suggested, it also facilitated the efforts of Porfirio Díaz to ensure a more compliant and less politically active judicial power in the years after Díaz's second reelection. The key to this control of the judicial power was Díaz's control of the electoral process itself and the constitutional requirement that justices be reelected every six years. In 1893 Díaz also defeated the attempt by the Liberal Union to bolster the independence of the Supreme Court by establishing a constitutional amendment granting the justices lifetime tenure.[2] Díaz is thus credited in most accounts that take up the period prior to the Revolution with eroding the decisional independence the Court had enjoyed during the period of the Restored Republic.

Most political and social historians of the Revolution would also agree with this last point. However, the place where the political historiography and the legal scholarship diverge relates to the period after 1917. According to most histories of the Revolution, Díaz's subordination of the judiciary is said also to have characterized executive-judicial relations after 1917. According to the legal scholarship on the judiciary, however, a new judicial power after 1917 gained an important margin of autonomy. Unlike most of the examples mentioned by Fix-Zamudio and others for the nineteenth century, however, the jurisprudence around the implementation of the new labor reforms, although it provoked the ire of certain state governments, triggered a far more ambivalent and cautious response from the authorities of the federal executive. It is not clear, then, that this was a jurisprudence that the federal executive strongly opposed, at least not prior to 1924. Indeed, the executive's switch to a more prolabor policy in 1924 happened during the Court's dramatic reversal of its original jurisprudence. This simultaneity lends support to political and social historians of the Revolution who have assumed that the Revolutionary-era Supreme Court was completely subservient to the executive branch of government on all important policy issues. Part of the task in what follows is to put the case for an important margin of judicial autonomy during these years on a stronger basis than it has hitherto enjoyed.

Another important theme, however, relates to the institutional scope of the Supreme Court's powers of amparo itself. As set out in the Constitution of 1857, amparo was originally intended to protect the Constitution's charter of individual rights and the federal structure; initially amparo was also restricted to the rights claims of private individuals. It was a classic formulation of liberalism's emphasis on negative rights in protecting a sphere of private autonomy.[3] Another distinctive feature of amparo was that even in the case of unconstitutional laws a favorable decision of the Supreme Court for the plaintiff provided relief only in that particular case (known in the doctrine as the "Otero formula") and did not extend to other individuals unless they also filed a suit of their own. This last characteristic has sometimes been interpreted by legal scholars and political scientists as so restrictive as to render amparo practically meaningless as a control of constitutionality. Although it is true that this system was far more indirect than the system of U.S. judicial review on which amparo was modeled in part, it was not so limiting as to prevent the Court from rendering legislation it felt conflicted with the Constitution a dead letter either before or after the Revolution. (This could not take place instantly, of course, but did occur over time with the accumulation of individual suits.) Indeed, it was sufficiently robust to be the constitutional power that was in question in several conflicts with other branches of government between 1917 and 1924.

Although the new constitution, best known for its innovations in agrarian and labor reform, was promulgated in February, a new Supreme Court did not begin functioning until June. New justices, elected on May 23, 1917, by a congress now dominated by the pro-Revolutionary PLC (Partido Liberal Constitucionalista, or Liberal Constitutionalist Party) majority, were also overwhelmingly drawn from the ranks of the victorious revolutionaries. In this respect the new Court was very different from the Supreme Court that had functioned between 1911 and 1914, on which a majority of justices had sympathized with forces hostile to the Revolution.

In 1917 three new justices, Alberto M. González, José María Truchuelo, and Enrique Colunga, were former constitutional deputies who had been responsible for raising social rights to the level of constitutional law earlier that year. González, who had also been a member of the special committee reporting on article 123, was active in the antireelectionist cause of Francisco Madero in 1910 and participated in the second revolution against Victoriano Huerta.[4] He eventually joined the forces loyal to Venustiano Carranza following the break between Villa and Carranza in 1914.[5] Prior to the Revolution Colunga had practiced law in Guanajuato. He was an associate of Francisco Lizardi, another constitutional deputy, but appears to have had no judicial (or other public service) experience during the Porfiriato.[6] Although none of the justices could be considered popular military leaders, at least two others, Enrique Moreno and Agustín Urdapilleta, had participated in the Revolution in some military capacity.[7] Prior to the Revolution Enrique Moreno had taught civil and criminal law at the Colegio Civil Rosales in the state of Sinaloa. In 1910 he joined Madero's antireelectionist cause (having previously been a Reyista) and fought in the battle for Culiacán in May 1911. He also took up arms against Huerta in March 1913.[8] Urdapilleta also joined the Madero revolution and was elected deputy to the legislature of his native state of Campeche. He took up arms against Huerta, achieving the rank of lieutenant colonel prior to his separation from the military in 1917. He also served for a short time as a military judge.[9] Another new justice, Santiago Martínez Alomía, was also from Campeche. He had served in various public posts during the Porfiriato, including deputy, representing Carmen, Campeche. He joined Madero's government in 1911 (as *abogado consultor de gobernación*).[10] He was also the brother of opposition journalist Salvador Martínez Alomía, director from 1913 to 1914 of *El Constitucionalista*, the official organ of the Constitutionalist revolution.[11] The new chief justice, Enrique de los Ríos, had been one of the official candidates of Madero's own Progressive Constitutionalist Party (Partido Constitucionalista Progresista) for Supreme Court justice in 1912. Madero, however, preferred an old stalwart of the Porfirian justice system, Demetrio Sodi, and Ríos was passed over in favor of Sodi.[12] Following his election to the new Supreme Court in 1917, Ríos reportedly told the press that he was a Revolutionary first and a Supreme Court justice second.[13]

The one obvious exception to a new Supreme Court made up of men who had been active in the Revolution against both Díaz and Huerta was Justice Victoriano Pimentel. Pimentel had even served the government of Huerta in one minor capacity, a stain on his record that in the eyes of many revolutionaries should have disqualified him from service in the new Revolutionary government. (Indeed, this issue became the topic of a heated debate in Congress on May 26, 1917, when Pimentel initially refused to accept his election to the new Court.)[14] Nonetheless, Pimentel's candidacy was strongly supported by radical Luis Sánchez Pontón and constitutional deputy Hilario Medina, both of whom advocated Revolutionary social legislation. Pimentel was probably also the only new justice who was widely regarded by the old Porfirian elite as a jurist in his own right. He also had some previous experience as a judge and public attorney, something that at least five of the new justices did not have.[15]

But if there were important differences between the Supreme Court that began functioning in June 1917 and the Madero Court of 1911–1913, there were also some important continuities. As already discussed, the Constitution of 1917 largely preserved the system of amparo as it had taken shape prior to the Revolution. (The most important innovation was the creation of the *amparo directo*, or amparo of a single instance, in cases filed against judicial sentences.)[16] The Revolutionary experience, said to be so important for shaping the new labor law, did not have an immediate impact on the amparo suit. Indeed, the obvious continuities linking amparo as it was practiced during the Porfirian era to the post-Revolutionary period allowed the new Supreme Court to admit and decide amparos filed since May 1917 despite the conspicuous absence of new regulatory legislation. In its accord of June 6, 1917, the first Court also ordered district-level judges appointed since the summer of 1916 to begin doing the same. These judges had been barred from doing so by a previous executive decree. As justice Santiago Martínez Alomía argued, the district judges should begin to process and decide these cases "in line with the Constitution and the previous legislation," to the extent that the latter did not conflict with the former.[17] It was, of course, the existence of a tradition of amparo and more than forty years of past experience as a constitutional court that made it possible for the new Court to proceed without waiting for new legislation, which, in any case, would not be passed by Congress until October 1919, that is, more than two years after the installation of a new Supreme Court.

The Court's Original Labor Jurisprudence

This decision on the part of the new justices was uncontroversial enough but it meant that they would also begin to hear amparo suits filed against the new social rights and the new labor law in particular. They would do so, then, under legislation passed in 1908 that, similar to previous legislation regulating amparo, established amparo as a suit of two instances: a first instance at the federal district level and a second (mandatory) revision of the first-instance decision by the Supreme Court in plenum. In those areas where there was no resident district judge, an amparo could also be initiated before a local "judge of first instance," or in urgent cases of life and liberty, any "justice of the peace" or other authority operating in an official capacity administering justice, provided that the competent federal judge (*juez de distrito*) be notified immediately. (Local judicial authorities, however, were barred from rendering "a final decision in these suits.") Because first-instance decisions were not carried out until the Supreme Court's final sentencing, the regulatory law also provided for the immediate "suspension of the act," which in special types of cases was an auxiliary action granted (or not) by the federal district judge or the above-mentioned local judicial authorities. Following the first-instance decision by the district judge, the entire case file was then forwarded to the Supreme Court, where final sentencing took place. ("Suspension of the act" proceedings were also forwarded and reviewed by the Supreme Court, which had five days to render a judgment but only if appealed by one of the parties to the suit or an injured third party.) The effect of a definitive sentence by the Supreme Court in favor of the plaintiff (in the case of unconstitutional "positive" acts) was to return things "to the state that they were prior to the violation," reestablishing for the plaintiffs "the full enjoyment of [their] violated constitutional right[s]."[18]

The first case decided in favor of a plaintiff against the new labor legislation was in an amparo suit filed by the company J. Crasseman. The responsible authority in the case was a new kind of constitutionally recognized institution, the boards of conciliation and arbitration (article 123, fractions XX–XXI). The facts of the case are as follows: an ex-employee of the company, Ignacio Guerra Casares, had filed a complaint for unpaid wages before the state of Yucatan's military commander. The commander, however, was not competent to decide the matter and referred the complaint to the Labor Department, which in turn passed it on to the recently created labor arbitration board. At the request of Guerra, the board petitioned the company for access to its account books, and though the company refused, the board persisted. The company, after failing to get the order stayed at the local level, filed amparo, citing a number of constitutionally guaranteed individual rights, including article 16.[19]

Three main points structured the Supreme Court's brief decision. The first was the question of whether the system of labor boards created by article 123 was intended to handle the conflict that had arisen between the company and its employee after the cited labor contract had lapsed. The Court answered this question in the negative, explaining, "[A]rticle 123 of the Constitution and the labor legislation in force treats laborers, wage workers, employees, domestics and artisans such that in the present case they are not applicable, from the moment when the aggrieved society, and the injured third party Ignacio Guerra Casares, no longer have the character of employer and worker respectively." Second, the Court did not consider the board's perceived need to see the company's books as part of the legally defined functions given to the boards by the Constitution. In the words of the decision, the main object of the boards was "to reconcile [*avenir*] employers and businessmen with the workers," and so by ordering the company to display its books against its will, the board had overstepped its legally circumscribed purpose. Third, the Court cited fraction XXI of constitutional article 123 as providing the employer, as well as the worker, the right to refuse to submit to arbitration before these administrative agencies. Therefore the board was not competent to force the company to comply with its request and consequently this authority had clearly violated in the person of the company the guarantee provided for in article 16 of the Constitution.[20]

Of the three points, it was the Court's interpretation of fraction XXI that was to have the most important repercussions for the subsequent functioning of the labor boards. This fraction read, "If the employer refuses to submit their differences to arbitration or to accept the decision pronounced by the board, the effect is the termination of the labor contract and he will remain obliged to indemnify the worker with three months' salary as well as the responsibility that results from the conflict. If the refusal is on the part of the worker the effect is the termination of the labor contract." For the Court, the decision to include sanctions for noncompliance implied that the decision to submit to arbitration was optional. Indeed, the possibility that the Constituent Congress had actually intended to create a system of labor boards that enjoyed the same powers as a tribunal, that is, jurisdiction with the power to pronounce sentences and make them respected, was, in the Court's own words, "inconceivable."[21] But it was not just the wording of article 123 itself that led the Court to refuse to recognize in the boards (an administrative, not a judicial entity) jurisdictional powers of a binding sort. There were also an important interpretation of article 16 and the division of powers at stake.

Certainly article 16 was not the only article cited by lawyers in their briefs or by judges in these early decisions, but it was the past precedent established around article 16 that most clearly conditioned the Court's interpretation. Article 16 as it existed prior to the Revolution was by all accounts the most adjudicated and probably one of the most effective constitutional rights claimed before federal courts in amparo proceedings. Moreover, it was article 16, far more than article 14, that had come to operate as a guarantee of the constitutional division of powers enforceable by the courts. This was one of the reasons given for retaining the most important wording of this article, despite, as already mentioned, multiple proposals for its amendment by the Constituent Congress of 1916–1917. According to Mexico's nineteenth-century jurists, article 16 provided, among other things, a guarantee of "constitutional competence," a concept that presupposed a particular understanding of "the nature of the public functions given the division of sovereign power for its exercise in legislative, executive and judicial power."[22] Though an examination of Mexico's constitutions (i.e., a study of legislation) might lead one to conclude that the theory of the division of powers has changed little over the past 150 years, a nineteenth-century liberal conception of this division differed profoundly from later welfare-state conceptions in at least one crucial respect. The line between the executive or administrative sphere and that of the judicial was mediated by a concept of "the contentious" (*contencioso*) that limited the actions of the executive branch in the (private) sphere of economic life.

In 1879, for example, the Supreme Court extended federal protection to Carlos Alvarez Rul and Luis Miranda é Iturbe against unconstitutional acts of the city government of the Federal District. The complainants had celebrated a contract with the city government on September 4, 1878, for the construction of several rail lines in the city. For reasons that do not appear in the published decision, the municipal government declared this contract null and void in March of the following year and, furthermore, ordered Alvarez and Miranda to remove all works already begun so as to return the streets to their original condition. Against these two administrative accords, Alvarez and Miranda filed amparo, citing among other violations those rights contained in article 16 of the Constitution.[23] The first Porfirian Supreme Court argued that a contract with a state authority was a special case, not reducible to civil law rules of contract and involving the public interest. However, it did not believe that these considerations justified the administrative authority's unilateral termination of this particular contract. Though there were several important exceptions enumerated by the Court, the majority did not feel that administrative authorities could decide matters of a contentious nature. Where the contentions began, so too did the jurisdiction of the courts, and in this way the courts limited the power of the executive. According to the Court, "[O]ne cannot declare that the lapse of the contract [*caducidad*] exists without resolving a matter of a contentious nature in which one has to define facts, apply the law relevant to the cause, and decide in this way a true litigation between the authority that sustains that this lapse exists and the concessionaires who deny that it does."[24] As a general rule, all contentious questions of rights were to be referred to the judicial branch. They could not be decided by the executive branch of government, and when the administration acted in these cases without first waiting for a judicial decision to resolve the contentious matter this was a violation of article 16's competency clause, actionable through amparo.

This interpretation as expressed in the Alvarez and Miranda case became a fixed feature of late nineteenth-century jurisprudence and the adjudication of article 16 in literally hundreds of cases.[25] Since Porfirio Díaz came to control the appointment of both judges at the district level and justices to the Supreme Court, it could easily be objected that this compliance with an older theory of constitutional competence was a merely formal exercise lacking the substance of a true system of checks and balances. Perhaps, yet even as a formal exercise, the national state's compliance with this jurisprudence was impressive. All the more so when we consider that this was a time of an important expansion of administrative bureaucracy and the increasing intervention of the national state in waters, lands, and mining and industrial policy.[26] On those occasions when the executive branch of government did overstep these limits as established by this jurisprudence, the assertiveness of the Court seems to have been unequivocal. In an amparo filed in 1896 over a dispute related to the declaration and survey of public lands, the Supreme Court told the Ministry of Development that, as an administrative body lacking "the constitutional jurisdiction for resolving contentious issues only to be resolved by the authorities of the Judicial Power, [the ministry's determination] violates the most generally established principles of jurisprudence."[27]

That this jurisprudence strongly conditioned the Supreme Court's initial interpretation of article 123 seems even more likely when we reflect on the debates of the Constituent Congress of 1916–1917. Indeed, one of the authors of the draft law that would later become article 123 was quite explicit on two important points: first, the main innovation of this particular draft law was the creation of a system of labor boards, and second, the labor boards were not to be considered tribunals.[28] For those justices who had been present during these debates, this was surely enough. The new labor boards were not to be regarded as an exception to the division of powers as traditionally understood and interpreted by the Supreme Court, which division limited the administrative sphere to the noncontentious.

A "Practical System" of Labor Arbitration?

Was it possible to sanction an important expansion of administrative power into the sphere of industrial relations and remain committed to a traditional interpretation of article 16? By the standards of twentieth-century welfare states this seems unlikely. It is my aim in what follows, however, to render this vision plausible by judging this jurisprudence not in the light of the modern administrative state as it would later develop but as the justices to the first Revolutionary Supreme Court understood it in the years 1917–1919. That the majority interpretation of the labor boards was not—as we shall see—an interpretation considered to be incompatible with the full implementation of a vigorous labor law also cautions us against imputing to it the predilections of an antilabor president or executive policy more generally. It is not beside the point to reiterate here that one of the main mechanisms of executive control of the judiciary was conspicuously absent in these early years, namely executive control of judicial appointments. Congress had the final say on Supreme Court appointments, and as we know from recent work on the history of the Chamber of Deputies, none of the early presidents effectively controlled the Congress.[29] Most importantly, however, it was simply not clear at the time what consequences the Court's early jurisprudence around article 123 would have.

Not only did the Court in its early decisions openly countenance all of the new principles and in general sanction the expansion of state power into the formerly "private sphere" of industrial relations, but if events had gone differently at the local level, it is quite possible that the Court's original jurisprudence would not have created a problem for implementation at all. This, then, would have been the first Court's "practical system" of labor arbitration as it was initially intended. In accordance with this self-understanding, fraction XVI recognized the right to form unions and the right of employers to form associations; fraction XVII stipulated that these associations could act coercively against each other using either the strike in the case of workers or the *paro* in the case of employers; fractions XVIII and XIX defined and limited these actions with additional restrictions placed on the paro. This kind of legal inequality was justified as an attempt to balance the economic power of employers, but wages (with the exception of the minimum wage) were still to be determined in a "market," albeit one in which collective bargaining was to play a decisive role. If fractions XVIII and XIX set forth the parameters for these new rules of the game, fraction XX created an organ to deal speedily and effectively with the conflicts that would inevitably arise from these new, legalized modes of direct action. Fraction XXI placed the burden of failed arbitration squarely on the shoulders of the employers.

The need for such provisions was, as the first Revolutionary Court explicitly recognized, a result of industrialism and the concentration of private power, which had resulted in the patent inequality of workers in their day-to-day relations with employers, a diagnosis with which Congress agreed. "The equality of the legal position of boss and worker" was the very first in a list of Revolutionary accomplishments presented by the Chamber of Deputies in the first draft labor law for the Federal District.[30] As in Europe, then, the new labor law found its principal justification in the changing social context brought about by industrialism. As one justice repeated before the Court,

> All of the justices know that the two characteristics of capitalist organization consist, first, in the concentration of work, in grand concentrations and, second, in the predominance of the capitalist over the workers. These two elements that are characteristic of the capitalist regime bring within an enormous injustice: that of breaking the equality of parts in a labor contract; the worker obliged by the necessity to live sacrifices his independence in order to receive a salary that permits him to live; the capitalist not by ill will, but by the necessary subjection to the inevitable principle of every capitalist business to obtain the greatest profit at the least effort and with the least cost, sacrifices the wage of the worker in favor of his profit; thus the worker who goes to agree to a contract submits himself to the necessity of living and ends up subjected to the will of the capitalist; from here the constant conflict between the worker and the capitalist. The new legislation, in its orientation toward social reform, has sought to create a means to guarantee the rights of workers in order that they can form part of human society [*la sociedad humana*], and the only means that they could find was to create an institution that has as its goal the prevention of those conflicts, making plain the right or the injustice of the worker when it goes beyond what it should and by making plain the need for the federal judiciary—to intervene to avoid such conflicts characteristic of the capitalist regime.[31]

Such an understanding would hardly have permitted a jurisprudence that intended to leave the labor boards without legal sanction. Indeed, their understanding of this sanction was in fact not much different from the one in force during the Weimar Republic, whose system of labor arbitration is still lauded by European scholars as a milestone in the history of labor law but is treated in Mexico as intentionally obstructionist and reactionary. The same justice explained,

> Justice González has already informed us of the sanctions that they have applied and explored in diverse countries of the world to make effective as possible the resolutions of the labor boards. For our part we have followed a practical system: When, in a conflict, one of the parts to the conflict does not want to submit to the basis of arbitration, this fact produces the following effects: first, it causes the rescission of the contract; consequently those that formed the labor

> contract are at liberty to comply with it . . . or not and should deduce their rights before the civil courts. Consequently, it is cause for indemnity in favor of the worker the fact that the employer has refused to comply with the contract. So that by the fact of the employer refusing to comply with the contract, the right to request three months' salary arises in the worker, but it is not the job of the Board of Arbitration to enforce this right. A right springs forth which *should be claimed before the tribunals.*[32]

This "practical system" envisioned by the Court was one that recognized in the boards the power to decide industrial conflicts in a manner that bypassed the formalities and delays of civil litigation. However, since the labor boards were administrative agencies, constitutional jurisprudence and sound constitutional interpretation dictated that their powers ceased whenever a private individual considered his or her private rights were being decided by an administrative action. In other words, though both the need and the social justification for the new labor provisions were recognized by the Court, the justices insisted that this new social demand also be reconciled with the constitutional interpretation of a delineated and limited division of powers as understood in the last third of the nineteenth century. To make the labor boards an exception to this conception of judicial control—in short, to recognize in the boards an "administrative tribunal"—would have been to undermine the constitutional guarantee contained in article 16, conserved unchanged by the Constituent Congress of 1916–1917.

Though various aspects of the Court's original jurisprudence on the constitutional competency of the new labor boards were contested by one or another of the justices at the time, there was nonetheless complete consensus with regard to the crucial question of the administrative nature of the labor boards and the limits imposed by a constitutional division of powers. They were not, to repeat, an exception to the constitutional interpretation of this division or article 16 of the Constitution. Any persistent doubts over this point are put to rest by an examination of the particular controversies that did divide the first Court in the early months of 1918.

In what appears to be the first sustained controversy over the juridical nature of the labor boards, the Court split over the question of whether these new agencies could be considered "authorities" for the purposes of amparo. If they were not, then the suit under consideration, filed by one Manuel Reyes, could not be admitted. Justice Pimentel, for one, thought that this particular position, sustained by Justice González and Justice Truchuelo, was simply untenable, though he did recognize the need to establish firm criteria on this question, since "we are going to continue to have many cases filed against the labor boards." He felt that "the boards of conciliation and arbitration do not have jurisdiction, that is to say, they are not tribunals, they are not judges that have the faculties to admit cases of litigants, of differences between private individuals and execute their resolutions; but that they do not have jurisdiction, that they are not tribunals, does not result in them not being authorities for the purpose of amparo."[33] Justice González disagreed, saying that the boards were "an auxiliary board to the administration." "[I]t has never been thought that they have public authority; in the case they are nothing more than arbiters and they have the duty of finding, as arbiters, *arbitradores* and *amigables componedores* in law. The decisions of the arbiters only have value between the persons or parties that subject themselves to the rules in the case. . . . [T]hey are subject to the requirements established by the Constitution because in this way one avoids the conflicts that could degenerate into an armed movement between employers and workers."[34] The majority agreed with González that both parties had to submit to make the resolutions binding, but it was Justice Pimentel's position that was to become the established jurisprudence of the Court. Although Justice Truchuelo also thought that the Court should stay (*sobreseerse*) this particular suit, he agreed with the majority when he said that those who are opposed to such a settlement do not have to simply accept it, "and then they go before the judge."[35] Despite being divided on the capital question of the suit's admissibility, all parties to the debate saw it as obvious that the boards could not treat contentious questions of right as if they were tribunals, a violation of constitutional article 16. Other aspects of the Court's original labor jurisprudence would be changed by a second Revolutionary court, installed on June 1, 1919. But these limits imposed on the labor boards would remain a central tenet of the judicial interpretation of constitutional article 123 until 1924.[36]

The Original Jurisprudence and the Rise of Organized Labor

The obstructionist consequences of this jurisprudence for the implementation of article 123 were not immediately obvious. Moreover, the obstacles that did arise were not exclusively the product of judicial decisions. The growing power of organized labor in state and national politics was also a contributing factor.

According to the labor historian Jeffrey Bortz, prior to the Revolution "unions were mostly not legal, often persecuted, and generally disdained by authority." There were none of the modern protections of labor law, and factory owners could count on the violent arm of the state to enforce their interests. [37] In 1906 and 1907 strikes were put down violently in the states of Veracruz and Sonora. With the Revolution, however, the legal status of workers and industrial workers in particular was vastly improved.[38] This did not happen to the same extent in every region, but the states where industrial violence was especially severe during the Revolution were also the states where workers became an important political constituency.[39]

One important factor in the rise of organized labor in Mexico, as elsewhere, was the creation of legal labor organizations. Mexico's first national labor organization, the Regional Confederation of Mexican Labor, or CROM (Confederación Regional Obrera Mexicana), was created in 1918, and a leader of one of the early electricians' unions, Luis Morones, was elected as its secretary general.[40] Under the leadership of Morones, the CROM plunged headlong into the political fray, signing a secret pact with presidential candidate Alvaro Obregón and founding a political party (the Labor Party) in order to launch candidates for national office. This was a significant break from the apolitical stance that the anarcho-sindicalist leadership of many of the early organizations had tried to maintain in electoral contests.[41]

Obregón's support was qualified, but there can be little doubt that the CROM gained strength with his ascendance to the presidency in 1920.[42] The CROM also benefited from its political links to Plutarco Elías Calles. Indeed, under Calles, Morones would be appointed minister of industry, commerce, and labor. During the early 1920s a Labor Party candidate also controlled the governorship of Mexico City for a time and six Labor Party candidates made it into the national legislature, including Morones himself.[43]

However, the real laboratories of revolution with respect to Mexico's nascent labor law were in the states and not in Mexico City. Although the various state laws were diverse (a principal complaint of industrialists lobbying for a national labor code), all of them privileged the labor boards as a central institution in the implementation of new social legislation. According to article 123, fraction XX, labor boards were required to have a tripartite structure, giving equal representation to employers and workers, with a deciding vote to be cast by a government official. This aided in the politicization of the workers' organizations, of which the CROM is the best (although by no means the only) example. The new unions had an important stake in controlling which workers were to be elected to the new labor boards. Unions with representation in the new state governments increasingly came to control the appointment of the presiding government official who could potentially favor the demands of one group of workers over those of workers belonging to a rival organization.[44] Under the new state laws, boards were charged with fixing minimum wage and profit-sharing arrangements, settling indemnities over work-related accidents, and perhaps most importantly, settling conflicts that arose over the labor contract. The 1918 Veracruz labor code even required a board's approval before an employee could be fired.[45] Large factories were also required to get approval before posting work rules regulating the shop floor.[46] Yucatan's new labor code made the decisions of the boards the one and only instance in any work-related conflict against which "no recourse is allowed."[47] In other words, they were the key institution charged with implementing the new social rights.

It is hardly surprising that those states with strong labor backing expanded the powers of this institution as much as possible, and this also explains why federal-state controversies on the question of the labor boards centered on the states that they did. As Kevin Middlebrook has concluded, "[T]he organization of conciliation and arbitration boards increased the labor movement's ability to translate its growing political importance into workplace gains."[48] In states like Yucatan, Veracruz, and Puebla, employers began filing suits against the decisions of local labor boards, and after 1918 they routinely received federal protection rendering these administrative actions null and void on the basis of the Court's established precedent. The Court decided against the administrative authorities even when they were acting within the bounds set by state law, declaring many of these new state laws unconstitutional.[49] Yet few of these state laws were changed to bring them into line with the Court's jurisprudence.

It is with this background in mind that we can begin to see how the Court's jurisprudence became the obstacle that it did. As organized labor pushed to expand the powers of the boards beyond the constitutional limits established by the Court, employers and industrialists, though alienated from the centers of political power, nonetheless found in the Supreme Court an invaluable tool for resisting the implementation of the new redistributive principles. The Court continued to decide these cases on the basis of its established jurisprudence of 1917–1918. In response, workers put direct political pressure on the Court to change its interpretation of article 123 and expand the constitutional powers of the boards. Protests were staged by organized labor, and both petitions and anonymous threats were addressed to the Court. Mexico City's press concluded that the Court's jurisprudence bore much of the responsibility for the current crisis around regulating and implementing the new labor law.[50] In the national legislature one deputy complained that "article 123 has been scandalously violated; in effect it is not in force, we all know it; it is the Supreme Court of Justice, to a significant degree, who is at fault since they have made the labor boards completely useless."[51]

Initially the political mobilization of labor and its threats of direct action foreclosed the possibility of a reconsideration of the Court's previous jurisprudence. The majority did not want to appear swayed by open political pressure or political intimidation. However, at least one justice broached the question of whether the justices should revisit their earlier position on the labor boards in response to workers' mobilization. In a discussion on January 30, 1922, with the Court already falling behind in its ability to decide the thousands of suits that were being filed against administrative officials, the majority moved to give preference to labor cases in order to speed their resolution. While not opposed to the initiative, Justice González (one of the few justices retained from the first Revolutionary Court) did object that the proposal did not go far enough. If the Court wanted to be responsive to the needs of the workers, he argued, it should not speed up the resolution of a handful of suits only to "protect an industrialist who doesn't want to pay three months' salary to the worker that he will fire."[52] He proposed that the Court consider recognizing the boards as tribunals, a position that he had first articulated in a dissenting opinion (*voto particular*) in the Dos Estrellas case, decided six months earlier.[53] Such a proposal, of course, meant an important modification of the doctrine of constitutional competence and the division of powers as guaranteed by article 16. The other justices, however, were not convinced. (Justice Moreno, also retained from the first Revolutionary Court, was to be especially emphatic on this point in the months that followed: "[T]he Court cannot give the boards more attributes than they have been given [constitutionally].")[54] It is significant, however, that this proposal came from Justice González, the same justice who in 1918 had elaborated on the "practical system" of labor arbitration originally intended by the Constituent Congress and had been opposed to the creation of labor tribunals.

Thus by 1922 there were an increasing number of reasons for the Court to reconsider one of the central postulates of nineteenth-century constitutional theory that had guided the early jurisprudence on labor. To begin, several of the assumptions that had supported this vision of a "practical system" were no longer plausible given the way the system had evolved in practice. For example, it had been widely assumed in 1917–1919 that the boards would eventually be perceived as benefiting owners and workers alike by providing an extrajudicial process that bypassed the delays associated with the local justice system, saving time and money and avoiding the costs of a strike. As with the newly sanctioned collective contracts, the public law that created the boards contained both carrot and stick, so that even though article 123 clearly benefited workers, it was argued, employers would soon find it in their interest to comply.[55] This was critical since the success of the system required the ultimate consent of both parties to make board decisions legally binding. However, in the case of the boards the incentives simply did not outweigh the costs and employers found it in their interest to avoid, in most cases, the intervention of the boards.

Another key assumption of the early jurisprudence was that workers would take an employer's refusal to submit to arbitration to the local courts. In practice this rarely happened. It is probable that the prospect of neverending litigation acted as a powerful deterrent to workers' civil suits.[56] Instead, workers and their unions continued to insist on the immediate enforcement of any resolution that came down from the labor authorities in favor of an individual or group of workers. In other words, they wanted the labor boards to have jurisdiction.

The Reversal of the Original Jurisprudence

It was the constitutional vision of the boards, promoted by the state legislatures and organized labor (especially the CROM), that would eventually triumph, though not until the appointment of a third Supreme Court. The election itself, drawn out over several months in the summer of 1923, was the most openly contested of the period, partly because these justices would now enjoy lifetime tenure but also because there was a significant fissure developing among various Revolutionary groups over the presidential succession of 1924. So severe was the contestation that it led to a stalemate between the Chamber of Deputies, which was controlled by the PNC (Partido Nacional Cooperatista, or National Cooperative Party) majority, and the Senate, during which time the Supreme Court ceased to function (its constitutional powers ending on June 1, 1923). Eventually the PNC majority reached a compromise with the Senate and was able to elect a majority of their candidates, reconstituting the Court on July 27, 1923, with several openly declared PNC favorites, including Francisco M. Ramírez, Jesús Guzmán Vaca, Manuel Padilla, and Ricardo B. Castro.[57] Only Ernesto Garza Pérez, former state congressman for Coahuila and secretary of foreign relations under Carranza, and Gustavo A. Vicencio, president of the Court from 1922 to 1923, were retained from the previous Court.[58] There is no evidence that the question of the labor boards was an explicit criterion for selecting these new justices (in fact, quite the opposite). Indeed, Victoriano Pimentel, one of the justices who was most responsible for the original jurisprudence, was not reelected to the Court in 1919 but was reelected in 1923. Also, Justice González, who openly declared for a reversal of the old jurisprudence between 1921 and 1923, was not reelected. Finally, those justices who were retained from the previous Court were initially against altering this established jurisprudence. By electing a majority of new justices, however, a new Supreme Court was to address this question of the labor boards with new eyes and at a time when the importance of the political support of organized labor had become a central feature of a new mass politics.

In December 1923 the crisis over the presidential succession had devolved into an open rebellion led by President Obregón's former treasury secretary, Adolfo de la Huerta, and key leaders of both the PNC and the PLC. A majority of the army had rallied to de la Huerta's cause and Obregón had been forced (albeit reluctantly) to rely heavily on irregulars such as armed campesino militias and the support of organized labor.[59] In the month of January, at the high-tide mark of the rebellion, the Court was faced for the first time with two cases that openly raised the question of the constitutional limits to the labor boards. The first of these was the Carlos Díaz Ordaz case, admitted by the Court by an eight-to-two majority vote on January 12, 1924, but reserved for substantive discussion at the first secretary's next turn.[60] On January 18, 1924, another case from Veracruz, this one filed by the Dutch-Mexican Company "la Corona," was brought for discussion before the Court. Since it presented similar questions of law as the Díaz Ordaz case, the Court voted to reserve "la Corona" pending a resolution of the earlier case.[61] On January 24, 1924, Carlos Díaz Ordaz was denied federal protection, as was "la Corona," settled one week later. Though both were unanimous decisions, the very different approach in interpretation and reasoning that the new justices brought to the question of the labor boards is especially clear in the transcripts of "la Corona" and its principal thesis.

The debate that took place between the old and new justices, culminating in the Court's February 1, 1924, decision to revoke the district judge's grant of federal protection, though not as apparent in the written argument itself, clearly reveals that the Court was willing to invest the boards with broad new powers, in effect making them administrative tribunals and giving their decisions the obligatory force of "the thing judged." Two new justices in particular, Justice Padilla, who had served the convention government in 1915, and Justice Castro, a former senator whose election to the Court had been sustained by the PNC, openly declared for a reconceptualization of the Court's old jurisprudence on the boards, a position questioned but not opposed by one of the justices who had been retained from the previous Court, Ernesto Garza Pérez.[62] According to the transcript, Justice Garza inquired whether there was in fact evidence that the executive branch had attempted to enforce the determination of the board against the complainants. If not, it was clear to him that the amparo could not be granted even on the basis of the previous jurisprudence and the decision of the district judge who had initially granted federal protection had to be revoked. For this reason, he suggested it was not necessary to go into the complexities of the Court's earlier interpretation of fractions XX and XXI of article 123. He then went on to explain the basis of the original jurisprudence and even to remind the Court that originally Justice González, a member of the Jacobin wing of the Constituent Congress, did not believe that the boards had the same powers as a tribunal. Yet he did leave the door open by suggesting that the old jurisprudence did not seem to adequately reconcile fractions XX and XXI to his satisfaction, an objection he was voicing aloud for the first time.

The decision itself appears to have been decided on the narrow legal question of whether or not the complainant had demonstrated through evidence that the board had in fact attempted to enforce its decision as well as the settled question of whether the boards were special tribunals prohibited by constitutional article 13.[63] However, the apparent willingness of a majority of new justices to recognize in the boards the power of "the thing judged," that is, their capacity to render binding decisions, when deciding a contentious question of conflicting rights signaled an important transformation in the Court's interpretation of article 123. The next day's headline in the Mexico City paper, *El Universal*, "The Boards of Arbitration will have the character of authorities [*autoridades*]," while only reiterating what had been a staple of the Court's jurisprudence all along, thus announced to the public the radical new stance the Court was about to bring to the question of the boards. The confusion of terms (the advocates of a radical new interpretation of the boards had spoken of *imperio*) highlights the extent to which the original basis of the Court's jurisprudence had come to be misunderstood or at least misrepresented and, therefore, the way Revolutionary public opinion had shifted, successfully pigeonholing the old jurisprudence as obstructionist and anti-Revolutionary. According to Justice Castro, "The truth is that if you negate authority and jurisdiction to the labor boards we would have to conclude that the Constituent Congress did not do anything to avert the conflicts between labor and capital."[64] The implication, of course, is that the justices who concluded otherwise must have been hostile to the interests of workers, setting forth a precedent that was intentionally obstructionist and counter to the intentions of the Constitution's founders. This is essentially the understanding of the Court's original jurisprudence that is remembered today.

Although there is no doubt that the 1924 reversal (recognizing "imperio") made the functioning of the boards immediately more effective in terms of vindicating the new social rights in favor of workers, it could do so only by suppressing what had previously been understood as a critical piece of liberal jurisprudence, one that had guided the work of both the Constituent Congress and the first Supreme Court. This was a transformation of constitutional law at least as significant and as far-reaching in its implications as many of the legislated changes made in 1917. As an early exception to an older conception of the division of powers, it provided one kind of legal answer for how an expanding administrative branch of government, being called upon to perform novel and conflict-ridden functions in the realm of economic life, was to be accommodated. Though this jurisprudence did not lead to a complete suppression of amparo of the sort that would come later in agrarian matters, it did carve out a large and important new sphere of administrative discretion in matters involving the rights of private individuals.

The system established by the new jurisprudence recognized in an administrative agency the power to pronounce sentences and ensure they were respected. However, the system of boards did not count on the judiciary's hierarchical system of appeal or its formal guarantees of procedure. Proofs were to be settled "in conscience," removing them from legal rules concerning use of evidence. The Court established jurisprudence that prevented the boards from applying the civil law in force in their state.[65] The Court also insisted that board decisions must be adjusted to the original complaint and the parties must be heard before such a decision was rendered, but this was the extent of any judicial-like requirements.[66] The anecdotal evidence suggests that cases were very much decided on a case-by-case basis with no regard for precedent and with frequent violations of the constitutional requirements that we would consider as central to a regime of due process.[67] For the workers, it mattered little whether the calculability that flowed from establishing precedent based on fixed legal rules, an intrinsic concern of bourgeois institutions of justice and Mexico's liberal jurisprudential tradition, existed as a feature of board's decisions or not.[68] What the workers did want was favorable decisions, and by the early 1920s, if not before, they knew that they could ensure such decisions through their newfound control of the political process. For employers, these new administrative "tribunals" were not tribunals of justice at all. Instead, what had before been the province of adjudication had now been converted into pure administration.[69]

The fact that this highly politicized reversal advocated by the new justices actually favored and complimented executive policy at the time, however, should not lead us to conclude that it was simply the foregone conclusion of a subordinated judiciary. The justices to the third Revolutionary Court not only possessed lifetime tenure, they had been appointed in part by President Obregón's opposition. It therefore seems unlikely (though we will never know for sure) that Obregón actually approached the Court prior to its January decision requesting a favorable resolution of this particular issue. On the one hand, it cannot be overemphasized that Obregón was occupied with an open rebellion that left him little extra time or motivation to negotiate with a majority of justices associated with the opposition over an issue that would have had little direct effect on the rebellion itself. The CROM's support was already committed and the Court, too, had promised to remain neutral in the conflict, even if the actions of several individuals implied otherwise.[70] On the other hand, those justices who were considered sympathizers with the opposition must have been well aware that this kind of decision would be interpreted favorably by the executive branch at a time when the tides were beginning to turn in favor of government forces.

In his 1929 article on the labor boards Narciso Bassols warned that by acting so freely "without adhering to defined norms," the boards might be serving the interests of labor presently, but without "a well-defined system of law," their dependence on the whims of the executive branch of government might turn against them.[71] As the next chapter describes, however, this continued defense of certain aspects of legal formalism on the liberal model as just as capable of benefiting the masses as the interests of the bourgeoisie was to become an increasingly minority position, at least among those who, like

Bassols, simultaneously sympathized with the realization of the new social rights. Among other things, this is because amparo, the most visible symbol of the formal guarantees that the Constitution extended to the individual, was to be continually used, even after 1924, by economic interests hostile to the social reforms contained in the Constitution. The increasing ability of landlords, for example, to obstruct the implementation of the agrarian reform in the second half of the 1920s was to reach crisis proportions.

How, then, was the new Revolutionary state to balance the escalating (and antiformal) demands for the rapid implementation of the new social rights with the requirements of a liberal Constitution as amended by the Constituent Congress? As we shall see in the next chapter, one of the answers given by the executive and legislative branches of government (though not by jurists like Bassols) was to temporarily suspend the constitutional rights of those affected by administrative acts in agrarian matters, though not until 1931 and only after a radical new precedent in administrative jurisprudence had been established by the Supreme Court.

CHAPTER FOUR

The Third Revolutionary Court and Legal Obstacles to the Implementation of Article 27

> The Court, by a brilliant jurisprudence, has juridically consecrated the rights conquered by the Revolution in favor of the workers; but it has not been able to do the same for the campesinos, for diverse reasons of resistance to the implementation of the most transcendental social program of the Revolution, which is the agrarian question.
>
> —Arturo Cisneros Canto, 1928

In an address prepared for the Academy of Legislation and Jurisprudence and read on January 13, 1931, Luis Cabrera estimated that, "prior to 1928, more than five thousand amparos have accumulated in the Supreme Court" against the agrarian reform.[1] Moreover, we know from an address to the Court by Justice Guzmán Vaca in 1928 that these amparos were being conceded at a rate approximating 75 percent.[2] These numbers are given in general terms, but taken together they give us a sense of the impasse that had developed between the Supreme Court, on the one hand, and the agrarian authorities, on the other, during the four-year term of President Calles.

More than any other issue, the new Supreme Court's increasing propensity after 1923 to grant judicial protection to landowners against the provisional land grant decrees of state governors and the definitive land grant decrees of the federal executive branch (known as dotación) seems to have facilitated the 1928 renovation of the very Court whose members, according to the Constitution, were now meant to be enjoying the guarantee of lifetime tenure. This was done as part of a sweeping set of constitutional reforms (also intended to fix a backlog problem of crisis proportions) to articles 94 and 96–100 initiated by Obregón on the eve of his reelection to a second (but nonconsecutive) presidential term. Although this constitutional amendment of 1928 seems to have tipped the balance in favor of those most committed to a radical shift in the Court's agrarian jurisprudence, it was not until the passage of two other amendments in 1931 and 1934 that Supreme Court intervention in this matter ceased to be an obstacle for the implementation of the agrarian reform and consequently an occasion for conflict with the executive branch.

The 1931 constitutional amendment to article 10 of the agrarian law of January 6, 1915, proved especially far reaching and completely barred those adversely affected by the redistribution of land from seeking redress in the courts. It may seem strange that a change to a preconstitutional law followed all of the requirements of a constitutional amendment, but this paradox is easily explained once it is recognized that the Court's agrarian jurisprudence, elaborated in the following pages, had interpreted this law as having been raised to the level of constitutional law by article 27.

According to the new article 10, however, "property owners affected by resolutions of dotación [land grants] and restitution [of usurped land] will not have any right or legal recourse, whether ordinary or the extraordinary one of amparo."[3] This amendment was to be repealed shortly after the massive acceleration of land redistributions carried out by President Lázaro Cárdenas, but it nonetheless represents an unprecedented suspension of what nineteenth-century jurisprudence had come to regard as one of the most important mechanisms guaranteeing the legality of a constitutional regime, namely judicial oversight through amparo.

As in the case of labor, a judge-made solution to problems generated around the implementation of the new social legislation required a significant reversal of principles related to past precedent and especially those principles related to a previous understanding of the judicial power's relation to the administrative branch of government. Unlike labor, however, the Court's jurisprudence was heavily influenced by the way the agrarian reform came to be regulated at the federal level by the executive and legislative branches, a factor that also seems to have mitigated against a judge-made solution prior to the judicial reforms of 1928. It is the continuity of legislative deference checked by a concern for judicial control that ultimately complicates the most obvious narrative, that of an antiagrarian judiciary from 1923 to 1928.

The Original Agrarian Jurisprudence

To understand why the Supreme Court became the obstacle that it did (and when it did) it is necessary to begin with the early agrarian jurisprudence established by the first Revolutionary Court, a jurisprudence that prior to 1920 did not involve any significant conflicts with the executive. In one of the first cases to reach the Supreme Court, for example, one Manuel Baigts filed amparo against a presidential land grant, or *dotación de ejidos*, in favor of the pueblo of Nazareno Etla, Oaxaca. Baigts's lawyers alleged that the complainant had been deprived of his best lands without notice or a hearing and that the agrarian authorities had not adjusted their acts to the applicable laws. In other words, constitutional rights set out in articles 14 and 16 had been violated.

In rejecting Baigts's claims and upholding the executive's definitive land grant, the first Revolutionary Court pointed out that the agrarian law of January 6, 1915, now formed an integral part of constitutional article 27 and that this preconstitutional decree clearly established an alternative and administrative procedure for the restitution and dotación of agrarian properties, one distinct from the due process guarantees referred to in articles 14 and 16. Since this law, reasoned the written decision of the Court, did not require that "the owners of the expropriated lands are given a prior hearing," then obviously "the legislature has not considered it necessary." It was therefore an "absurdity" that "the complainant sustains that this should have been done, invoking a different constitutional text," and thus attempting "to destroy the exception, with help from the general rule."[4]

The Court's reluctance to require of this new administrative procedure compliance with such fundamental rights of the past as prior notice and a formal hearing should give moment for pause, and it seems to signal that the first Revolutionary Court was indeed sympathetic to the cause of redistributive social rights. As with labor, however, the Court did not rule out judicial intervention in the process altogether. Thus in the Baigts case, as in later cases, the Court retained the power of judicial oversight. This was to include holding the administrative authorities accountable to the applicable law and judicial evaluation of the facts relevant to the case, a much more expansive notion of judicial control than the common-law interpretation of ultra vires that was soon to characterize judicial control of administrative acts in the British welfare state.

Initially, however, the only legislation in force regulating the acts of the administrative authorities was the preconstitutional agrarian law of 1915, which, as I have already said, was recognized by the Court as part of article 27, that is, part of the Constitution. In the early years after 1917 the Court was adamant that it would not grant amparo for a violation of articles 16 or 14. Instead, amparos granted against the early agrarian reform were always for violations of article 27. Article 27 set out three important constitutional limits to the implementation of the agrarian reform. These included the protection of the "small property" (*pequeña propiedad*) and, in dotación, or land grant, proceedings (which quickly surpassed the number of restitutions since the burdens of proof were far less stringent), the requirement that these population centers demonstrate a need for the land and that the land they had received was taken from "adjacent" (*inmediatas*) estates.

Nonetheless, the Court rarely granted amparo against the early agrarian reform (which in any case began rather slowly), and this despite its recognition that it did have a role to play in overseeing the legality of administrative action. It is possible that with different members the Court on the basis of the same jurisprudence may have found more cause to intervene against the agrarian reform during these years, but the Court's deference to the administrative authorities was also facilitated by the lack of more extensive regulatory legislation, which might have more completely specified the content of those legal limits set out in article 27 (something that did take place later).

A case in point is the Amparo Enrique G. de Salceda, filed against the agrarian authorities for a land grant decree favoring the town of San Pedro Totoltepec in the state of Mexico. De Salceda was the owner of a large estate (la hacienda Doña Rosa) but he attempted to convince the Court that his expropriated lands should be protected as a small property. Article 27 defined *small property* as anything smaller than fifty hectares for the purposes of restitution. However, it was silent on the question of whether the same definition applied to dotación proceedings of the type that had resulted in the expropriation of de Salceda's property. Moreover, the twelve short provisions of the agrarian law of January 6, 1915, provided little guidance on this particular point. Despite this ambiguity, the Court did not think that de Salceda's large estate could be considered a small property.

But the Court took much more seriously the complainant's other claim about the estate's proximity to the pueblo of San Pedro. As Justice Truchuelo suggested, the expropriated property was not (strictly speaking) "adjacent" (inmediata) to the community receiving lands. On these grounds alone he felt the Court should grant protection to de Salceda. Justice Urdapilleta disagreed and suggested that "adjacent" in this context should be interpreted to mean close by (*inmediatos o cercanos*). A similar requirement in article 3 of the agrarian law, however, was far less amenable to this kind of interpretation. Instead of just using the word "adjacent" (inmediata) this article mandated that expropriations be "directly adjacent" (*inmediato colindante*), which seemed to suggest a shared border. Justice Urdapilleta, however, reasoned that the difference in wording between the two laws implied that "the Constitution has changed the terms [of the original law] using the word 'adjacent' [inmediatas] and suppressing 'directly adjacent' [inmediatas colindantes a los pueblos]." Because the Constitution was supreme, it therefore nullified this aspect of the earlier law and consequently amparo could not be granted on these grounds.[5]

Justice Urdapilleta's innovation in this regard appears to have been motivated by his concern that the pueblo in question would not be eligible to receive any lands should the Court grant amparo. From the documents before them, it was evident that this community was surrounded on all sides by properties much smaller than de Salceda's. Did this mean, asked Justice de los Ríos, that even though the community's need for land had been demonstrated, it would be ineligible for land simply because it was surrounded by small properties? What would happen to those in need if the Court granted amparo? Was it right to nullify this land grant and protect an estate whose size clearly violated the spirit of article 27 just because it did not share a border with the town of San Pedro? The majority of the Court sided with the argument of Justice Urdapilleta and denied amparo to the complainant despite the fact that his property was not "directly adjacent," as specified in article 3 of the agrarian law.

One interpretation of the above case, then, is that the contradictory nature of early agrarian legislation allowed the Court to be extremely flexible in its approach to the agrarian reform. Although the regulation of these provisions was given a high priority by many of the delegates to the first federal Congress (a draft law had already passed the Chamber of Deputies by 1918), it was not until the regulatory law, or *reglamento*, of 1922 that a limit like the "small property" was defined in such a way as to fix its meaning for both the administration and the Court in land grant proceedings.[6] Moreover, the unwillingness of the Supreme Court to grant protection in cases like the Amparo

Enrique G. de Salceda suggests that the majority were in fact ideologically committed to the realization of agrarian reform. Even those who argued in favor of extending judicial protection to the complainant in the case just discussed cannot be considered sympathizers to the landlords' cause. Justice Truchuelo, for example, was to be a leading proponent of both agrarian and labor reform in his home state of Querétaro in the years after 1919.[7]

From 1917 onward, the Court established that in all suits filed against the agrarian reform the immediate suspension of the act was *not* to be granted by the district judge, a matter of course in most other administrative cases.[8] (This meant, among other things, that those who had just received land would continue to legally hold it while the suit made its way through the federal justice system, a process that could take months and sometimes years.) The Court also facilitated the ability of administrative authorities to allow dotación to a community on the basis of a failed petition for restitution without requiring the initiation of a separate process.[9] The right to private property was explicitly rejected by the Court as an absolute right and in the context of the agrarian reform they allowed the taking of land without a prior indemnity or even an estimation of its value, two requirements that would have resulted in grants of federal protection by the Supreme Court during the Porfiriato.[10] According to Justice Martínez Alomía of the first Revolutionary Court, "Our Constitution has reformed property in such a way that it has been subordinated to the collective need in place of being an absolute and exclusive right of the individual."[11] And as Chief Justice Enrique Moreno explained to Obregón in 1921, the agrarian jurisprudence of the Court, although it had occasionally ruled against the president, was in agreement with those who felt at the time that property could no longer be treated as "an end in itself." A new understanding of the right of property had emerged that treated property as a "means to achieve an object," which, according to Moreno, was none other than "increasing the general wealth, contributing in this way to social utility."[12]

By 1921 these ideas were neither new nor revolutionary. They had been widely disseminated by, among others, the well-known French jurist Léon Duguit, whose writings now shared a prominent place in the curriculum at the National School of Jurisprudence in Mexico, thanks to the work of Manuel Gómez Morin.[13] However, the kind of agrarian reform that these ideas now sanctioned was new, and in the first five years of the Constitution's tenure the Supreme Court actively encouraged the administrative branch of government to do what it felt was necessary to alter the land tenure arrangements of rural

Mexico, a reform the Court cast in terms of public utility. So what changed after 1923? Besides a new Court, the main factor behind the Court's increasing propensity to grant amparo to affected landowners was the way the agrarian reform was regulated after 1922.

Legislative Change and Constitutional Interpretation

Although secondary legislation that more completely regulated the agrarian reform was first promulgated in December 1920, scholars of this period have generally recognized that it was not really until the regulatory law (reglamento) of April 1922 that order was brought to the complicated framework that had guided legal practice. As Paul Friedrich has written, it was the regulatory law of 1922 that, much more than the law of ejidos of 1920, greatly facilitated "a way through the legal tangle for agrarian leaders."[14] Thus the new regulatory law provided a remedy to a situation that by all counts had become intolerable because of the indeterminate and even contradictory nature of forty-some executive circulars decreed since 1916 and the silence of the agrarian law of 1915 on many important issues.

The new regulatory law specified the amount of land each petitioning individual or head of family should receive; it defined both restitution (articles 4–8) and dotación (articles 9–23) in much the same terms as the original agrarian law of 1915; it reintroduced the possibility of provisional grants by state governors (provisional grants had been suppressed by the law of ejidos of 1920); and it sought to curb unnecessary delays and corruption by fixing the periods of time that each step in the process could take, which had already begun to tarnish the reputation of official agrarian reform in the eyes of those who were most intent on realizing this most revolutionary of promises.

It was also this new regulatory law, however, that was largely responsible for the increasing ability of landlords to file successful suits against the agrarian reform. According to Ignacio Burgoa, it was not really until the years 1923–1927 that the Court's agrarian jurisprudence admitted and granted amparo for violations of articles 14 and 16, and this clearly seems to have been prompted by the new way the agrarian procedure was regulated.[15] Among other things, the law extended several quasi-judicial guarantees to affected landowners, giving them a legal voice during the creation of the "agrarian file" and stipulating that they be heard prior to the expropriation of their property by a definitive presidential resolution. In 1917 the first Revolutionary Court had rejected these very same requirements as unnecessary. This changed with the 1922 regulatory law. "In effect, a procedure that had previously been purely administrative, expropriatory with respect to the properties of the affected lands and a simple matter of bureaucratic steps concerning only the soliciting centers of population and the agrarian authorities," Lucio Mendieta y Núñez has written, "was transformed into a truly judicial conflict before administrative authorities." The Court now perceived the agrarian reform through a new lens—as a contentious procedure in which competing rights were in play.[16]

In one of the first cases decided by the Court after the promulgation of the new regulatory law in 1922, the Court granted amparo to Ana Fernández viuda de Sela against a dotación de ejidos to the pueblo of San Mateo Ayecac by a seven-vote majority.[17] According to the complaint, the agrarian authorities had violated article 27, fraction III, which protected properties of less than fifty hectares. The agrarian authorities had also violated article 16 because the president did not "legally motivate the cause of procedure," and this was especially so since the president's grant was not, according to the complainant, a dotación or restitution but an extension, or *ampliación*, of a previous land grant, an action that had no basis in the agrarian law of 1915. Finally, the agrarian authorities had violated article 14 because the National Agrarian Commission had not deemed it necessary to give the complainant a hearing. The agrarian authorities, for their part, responded that Fernández was actually the owner of a large estate but that she had attempted to avoid expropriation by dividing and selling pieces of this estate in February 1918, a sale the executive branch had declared null and void.

The Court agreed with the agrarian authorities to the extent that it rejected the alleged violations of articles 14 and 16. With respect to whether or not the agrarian authorities had a legal basis for granting the so-called extension, or ampliación, of ejido lands, the Court declared that this was simply a "question of words, and that to extend [ampliar] the ejidos of a pueblo was equivalent to granting the same with more lands." It thus was a faculty delegated to the administrative branch of government in the original agrarian law of 1915. Nonetheless, the majority did not defer to the executive branch, as it had done in the past, on the question of whether the complainant's lands should be considered a small property, and it was, therefore, the alleged violations of article 27 that the Court used to justify its decision in favor of the complainant. First, the Court agreed with the complainant that the executive branch did not have the power to nullify the sale of her lands, even though this sale probably followed the initiation of the agrarian proceedings in favor of the pueblo.[18] Second, the Court argued that since this sale could not be unilaterally declared null and void by the executive branch, the complainant's property clearly constituted a small property, warranting its constitutional protection. The Court acknowledged that at the time of the presidential resolution the term *small property* had not yet been "defined in a precise manner." However, the Court noted that at the very least, in cases of restitution article 27 recognized the number of fifty hectares, a minimal definition of a small property. The executive reaffirmed the fifty-plus hectares definition in article 14 of the new regulatory law, with gradations for poor-quality land, using the following distinctions: anything less than 150 hectares for irrigated lands or lands of abundant rainfall should be considered a small property; anything less than 250 for lands where rains were seasonal but "regular and abundant"; and anything less than 500 for lands of seasonal rainfall of other classes.

Perhaps the clincher for the majority of the Court, however, was that in a separate agrarian file involving a separate land grant procedure to the pueblo of San Lucas Atoyatenco, the agrarian authorities had considered the property of the complainant as a small property. "Surely," concluded the written decision of the Court, "this antecedent cannot be considered as having the characteristics of exception by *cosa juzgada* [the thing judged], since it does not relate to the same pueblo; but this resolution constitutes, by itself, a powerful argument in favor of amparo for violation of the third paragraph of article 27 several times cited."[19]

Although the regulatory law was not considered applicable to this particular case, it nonetheless influenced the Court's decision by specifying the legal content of article 27's protection of a small property. This was also an important factor in a decision of June 18, 1926, in which the Court confirmed the district judge of Tlaxcala's decision to grant amparo to Antonio Zamora Carrasco and associates against a presidential land grant for a violation of the third paragraph of article 27, that is, as small-property owners as defined by the new regulatory law.[20] The district judge had argued that even though article 27 had not defined precisely what constituted a small property in dotación proceedings, the regulatory law of 1922 clearly did. There were, however, different categories of small property, and while the agrarian authorities had determined that the affected properties of the complainants should be included in article 14, fraction II (lands in which rainfall was "regular and abundant"), the district judge disagreed, considering the complainants' lands covered by fraction III (seasonal rainfall of third class). But even if the complainants' lands were protected only by fraction II, the district judge asserted, this would not be sufficient grounds for denying amparo since the complainants' land had been divided into three pieces, each smaller than the maximum as set out in article 14, fraction II, of the regulatory law.

In requesting the Supreme Court's revision of the case, the public attorney (*ministerio público*) and the National Agrarian Commission complained that it was not true that the lands in question were a small property protected by article 27 since they exceeded the limit of fifty hectares, and the division into three fractions (corresponding to three different individuals) cited by the district judge was irrelevant because the property was still held jointly (pro indiviso). They also questioned the ability of the complainant (and the judge) to dispute the content of the technical reports made on behalf of the administration for the purposes of the agrarian file (in this particular case with respect to the amount of annual rainfall).

The Supreme Court agreed with the agrarian authorities that the district judge had been incorrect to assert that the property in question had been divided into three fractions since the fact that the property was still held jointly had even been recognized by the complainants in their original brief. However, the Court did not agree with the argument of the administrative authorities that the complainants had no right to dispute the technical reports used in assessing which properties were or were not to be affected in the course of a dotación proceeding. The Court did not agree because article 28 of the new regulatory law required that "[i]n every file involving restitution or dotación de ejidos, the authorities will attach and consider all of the proofs and writings that the affected landowners present and once the respective steps have been taken the authorities will notify these, the affected landowners, who will have thirty days to present before the National Agrarian Commission those arguments that in their right they deem convenient." To therefore prohibit the complainants from challenging the assessments made in the technical reports, argued the Court, would be to restrict unnecessarily "the right to a defense that corresponds to the property owner." Moreover, from the documents submitted in the course of the suit, "it appears that the pluvial precipitation on this farmland is regular but not abundant, from which one can deduce that this farmland is not to be included in fraction II, but in fraction III of article 14 of the regulatory law."[21] Consequently, the complainants' property should not have been affected by the agrarian authorities as part of the president's resolution of February 20, 1924, giving lands to the pueblo of Santa Ursula Zimatepec.

The Court handed down a unanimous decision in which all eleven justices were present.

However, the regulatory law did much more than just specify the content of the small-property restriction (articles 14, 15, and 17). In articles 18, 19, and 20 the regulatory law also introduced other restrictions, including the protection of fruit trees and cash crops such as vanilla, coffee, and rubber and the protection of irrigation works instrumental to nonaffected lands. Article 19 allowed for a certain period of time in which affected landowners could harvest their crops prior to provisional or definitive possession by the soliciting pueblos, and article 20 gave these owners the option of substituting lands planted with "cyclical crops" for those of equal value elsewhere as long as their location was no more than five kilometers from the soliciting population. All three of these articles formed the basis for successful suits during the years in which the regulatory law was in force, with violations related to article 18 being the most common, at least as far as the published record is concerned.

Article 28 of the regulatory law gave affected landowners intervention in the creation of the agrarian file through its requirement of notice and a hearing, a requirement that also existed for the formulation of the original agrarian census as set out in articles 12 and 22 of the same law and that also proved cause for grants of judicial protection by the Supreme Court. In a decision of August 21, 1926, for example, the Court conceded amparo to Ignacio Ruiz de Chávez for the following reasons:

> First—the complainant is owner, since April 14, 1924, of a part of land that belonged to the hacienda de "Pilotos," property of Mr. Carlos Arellano Valle: second—the respective deed was inscribed in the Public Register of the city of Aguascalientes on May 14 of the same year: third—on February 4, 1925, the neighbors of "Rancho Seco" solicited ejidos, forming the respective file and leading to its provisional grant decreed by the Governor of the State with the date of March 29 of the same year of 1925, which distributed four thousand hectares to the congregation of that name which they took from the hacienda of "Pilotos": fourth—that in this file, they only gave intervention to Mr. Arellano Valle, but not to Mr. Ignacio Ruiz de Chávez: and fifth—in sum, that this man was dispossessed of that property in executing the expressed resolution of the Executive of Aguascalientes. Hence, the reclaimed act is true consisting in the fact

> of having stripped the complainant of the possession of the land of reference, without hearing him . . . and the unconstitutionality of this act is evident because it contravenes the guarantee provided for in constitutional article 14 that proclaims, "no person shall be deprived of life, liberty, property, possessions or rights without due process of law instituted before a duly created court, in which the essential elements of procedure are observed and in accordance with previously existing laws." In the case, intervention should have been given to Mr. Ruiz de Chávez, a property owner of part of the lands affected with the dotación conceded to the neighbors of "Rancho Seco," in compliance with articles 12 and 22 of the regulatory law, and having not done this, they did not apply these precepts or hear them in their defense of the property affected by the dotación, violating in their person the expressed guarantee.[22]

Just two months earlier the Court had explicitly rejected a complainant's appeal to constitutional article 14, arguing that "said violations do not involve an infraction of constitutional article 14 because this article refers to suits filed before the tribunals, which in agrarian matters do not have constitutional jurisdiction."[23] This was in keeping with the jurisprudence of the first Revolutionary Court. Thus the fact that the Court seems to have changed its position on this important point (granting amparo for violations of both articles 14 and 16 on a regular basis after 1926) seems to indicate a new conservatism on the part of the Court toward the agrarian reform. But it would be wrong to consider the third Revolutionary Court as somehow more conservative on the question of Revolutionary social reform than the first. (Chapter 3 argued that the third Court conceived of itself as much more revolutionary than the first.) Despite the shifting constitutional basis for grants of federal protection against the agrarian reform, there seems to be something of an underlying continuity. Indeed, it is this underlying continuity more than the shifting constitutional basis for successful grants of judicial protection that set the third Revolutionary Court on a collision course with the agrarian authorities of the executive branch.

What most exasperated the justices on the third Revolutionary Court, even those who would later be responsible for a radical new jurisprudence in agrarian matters, was that the administration increasingly violated the applicable agrarian legislation. Moreover, the laws in question were overwhelmingly the work of the same branch of government that was violating them. If these rules were the will of the executive branch, the norms of which ought to guide administrative action, then the Supreme Court was obliged by the very nature of its functions to intervene and prevent wrong (administrative) decisions. What was exasperating, then, was the idea that the Court could possibly do otherwise. This type of correction of administrative error was considered central to the functioning of amparo and the Supreme Court's powers of judicial control as these had been understood and consolidated prior to the Revolution.

On the one hand, both Obregón and Calles, although they were not radical agrarians, most likely realized the value of a selective agrarian reform as an instrument of political power. They were certainly the beneficiaries of a selective reform during such state crises as the Delahuertista revolt in 1923, the Cristiada uprisings in western Mexico during the second half of the 1920s, and the 1927 revolt led by Calles's secretary of war, Francisco Serrano, and Gen. Arnulfo R. Gómez. Indeed, Calles granted 3,045,802 hectares as president and Obregón approximately 1,556,983 hectares.[24] On the other hand, precisely because they were not radical agrarians, they presided over a proliferation of regulatory laws that revealed the conservative tendency implicit in their productivist vision for a new Mexico.[25] (Obregón, in particular, was extremely reluctant to divide large landed estates that were productive, going concerns.) This difficulty was implicitly recognized by the agrarian authorities themselves, who at times seemed to have no other recourse than to argue that the secondary legislation in force (especially the regulatory law of 1922) was only selectively applicable and it should be left to the discretion of the administration to comply with it or not, an argument that the third Revolutionary Court (in keeping with earlier jurisprudence) found unacceptable.

In one such case, for example, the agrarian authorities acknowledged that their procedure had violated article 1 of the new regulatory law, which required of the petitioning communities a certain "political category," really a census designation, in order to receive lands. However, they did not believe that an amparo should be granted on these grounds alone and they suggested that "the confirmation of the political category [as set out in article 1 of the new regulatory law] was a trivial requirement of mere form." The Court disagreed, explaining, "[I]t is clear that one cannot consider trivial and of mere form the requisites that the same President of the Republic has felt to be indispensable to the right to ask for lands, as expressed in the regulatory law that the same high functionary decreed as the norm in land grant proceedings."[26]

On another occasion the authorities went as far as to argue that the regulatory law was unconstitutional in its entirety and therefore could not be applied by the Supreme Court in evaluating the legality or illegality of administrative acts. The Court responded to this argument by saying that they found it very perplexing that "the National Agrarian Commission, which, in the case, is the constitutional organ of the federal executive, objects to the validity of the regulatory law that this same authority has passed." Because transitory article 11 of the Constitution gave the president the power to regulate the agrarian reform, the validity of the regulatory law was beyond doubt.[27]

This, too, would have caused considerable consternation on the part of the justices on the first Revolutionary Court, even though they did not think articles 14 and 16 were applicable to the agrarian reform. That the third Revolutionary Court began to apply articles 14 and 16 in agrarian cases after 1926 had more to do with the changes brought about in agrarian procedure by the secondary legislation than anything else. Indeed, given the way the regulatory law had evolved over time, the idea that agrarian procedure should comply with articles 14 and 16 was no longer seen as problematic—a point emphasized by the principal author of the Agrarian Code of 1927, Narciso Bassols.[28] Nonetheless, an acceleration of the agrarian reform under Obregón and Calles co-occurred with an increasing number of legal requirements set out in the secondary legislation that the administrative authorities increasingly proved unable or unwilling to meet. The Court granted amparo and did not think it could do otherwise.

Already in April 1925, Justice Vicencio felt that it was necessary to protest to the president that the Court's decisions against land grant and restitution proceedings did not involve a conflict of criteria between these two branches of government. Several newspapers in Mexico City suggested otherwise, and Vicencio's letter to the president was published as an open letter in response to several sharp criticisms of the Court.[29] Vicencio's letter reflected the consensus on the Court that the Court's agrarian jurisprudence was not reactionary or counter-Revolutionary but was in keeping with the most basic principles of a state of laws, indispensable for the legitimacy of the new Revolutionary state. The Court was only holding the executive branch to the applicable law. In another interesting exchange with President Calles a year later, Justice Padilla assured the executive branch that the Supreme Court would start doing a better job of keeping the president informed of all pending agrarian cases. Attached to the note was a recent circular of the Court that had been motivated by a request from Calles. It required all district judges to keep the executive branch informed of "amparo suits that are filed against presidential resolutions in agrarian matters."[30] Yet the good relations that Vicencio and Padilla tried to maintain with the executive branch could hardly conceal the fact that the Court was becoming a significant obstacle to the swift resolution of the agrarian problem. As of January 1925, more than 1,400 amparos filed against the agrarian reform were pending before the Supreme Court; the Court would grant close to 200 amparos against dotación and restitution proceedings (including definitive presidential land grants) prior to its forced renovation at the end of 1928.[31]

The new Agrarian Code, promulgated in April 1927, was motivated to a large degree by this impasse, and it attempted to deal with some of the worst problems with the 1922 regulatory law as these had come to light through practice. Perhaps its principal innovation was its removal of the earlier law's use of census categories as a juridical tool for assessing the eligibility of petitioning communities (i.e., their "political category"), carried over from the law of ejidos of 1920. According to Luis Cabrera, this requirement, as set out in articles 1 and 2 of the regulatory law, had been the leading cause for successful grants against the agrarian reform.[32] That is, nowhere was the administration's disregard for the letter of the regulatory law more significant than with respect to article 1's requirement that all petitioning communities had to have the political category of either "pueblo, ranch, congregation, condueñazgo or community." Frequently the populations most in need of lands did not fit within one of these categories for reasons having to do with the nomenclature employed by the various states, and consequently the National Agrarian Commission found itself recommending land grants to populations that did not fall into the appropriate political category or had not been categorized (a power reserved to the state legislature) at all.

Although the new law eliminated this requirement, which Bassols argued was an unfortunate innovation of the law of ejidos of 1920, it did not reverse or undo the quasi-judicial safeguards extended to affected property owners. Indeed, the law represented a new level of systematization in this respect, establishing beyond doubt certain essential forms of procedure that were to be applied in every case. According to Bassols (summarizing the requirements of the new law), a petition or suit for land must be "initiated through a solicitation by the village settlement," without sufficient lands. Prior to rendering a verdict, the agrarian authorities must allow "for the intervention of all those affected, providing for the discussion and verification of the relevant data," including: legal "proof" that the need for land is real, "that there are agriculturalists and individuals capable of doing agriculture once land is obtained," and "that they are not owners of lands," "either because the pueblo does not have them, or because those that they have are not sufficient." In brief, Bassols envisioned the new agrarian procedure as "a suit before administrative tribunals [*tribunales administrativos*] with two instances, with a well-defined process of substantiation, and that closes with a sentence that fixes the allocation [*afectación*] in such a way that it cannot be changed.[33]

Although, as Mireya Toto has noted, "there is no doubt that this law represents an advance" over all previous agrarian law, it is also true that the Agrarian Code of 1927 represents a continuation of the trend, denounced by many agrarians at the time, toward a judicialization of an administrative process, discerned in the 1922 regulatory law, and in the short run its innovations did little to stem the actual tide of successful suits being granted by the Supreme Court against the reform.[34] For the most part, the suits that the Court was deciding in the years immediately following the promulgation of the new law concerned agrarian files closed prior to April 27, 1927, and therefore concerned the application (or violation) of the regulatory law of 1922.

By the time the federal Congress was asked to decide whether the present Court was going to continue to enjoy the guarantees against executive interference put in place by the original charter of 1917, it had become a significant obstacle to the implementation of an agrarian reform. As one of the principal proponents of a new agrarian jurisprudence complained in 1928, "The Court, by a brilliant jurisprudence, has juridically consecrated the rights conquered by the Revolution in favor of the workers; but it has not been able to do the same for the campesinos, for diverse reasons of resistance to the implementation of the most transcendental social program of the Revolution, which is the agrarian question."[35]

The Constitutional Amendments of 1928

This larger context is crucial for understanding Obregón's successful bid to end the lifetime tenure of the third Revolutionary Court and ensure executive control over the judicial appointment process. Obregón was considered at the time to be more sympathetic to agrarian reform than many of his rivals, and he was strongly supported in his reelection efforts by the National Agrarian Party, or Partido Nacional Agrarista, led by, among others, such former Zapatistas as Antonio Díaz Soto y Gama. Although the constitutional reform of articles 94, 96, 97, 98, 99, and 100 was also couched in terms of expanding the capacity of the Court to deal with the problem of a severe backlog of cases, responsible for delays in the administration of justice, there were many different ways this problem could have been handled that would not have required the increasing predominance of executive control over the judicial branch of government.

Indeed, the very importance that Obregón attached to this reform seems to indicate his continued unease about the previous actions of the Court and its current membership. And as the debates over this proposed constitutional reform clearly reveal, it was not just a concern for the efficient administration of justice that motivated those who supported Obregón's proposed constitutional reforms. Not only were partisan conflicts heightened because of the political battle around Obregón's reelection, flaunting one of the most important political reforms of the Revolution (the constitutional prohibition on reelection), but in a departure from previous debates over this question, the deputies were especially hostile toward the present membership of the Court, a tendency likely reinforced by its association with the Congress of Prieto Laurens, one of the leaders of the Delahuertista revolt in 1923 (see chapter 3).

The debates that took place in the Chamber of Deputies over the passage of these reforms are especially revealing for their rejection of the constitutional theory of the Supreme Court that had guided the work of the Constituent Congress of 1916–1917.[36] In a speech delivered on May 18, 1928, the laborite Vicente Lombardo Toledano defended the liberal principles enshrined in the unreformed Constitution, arguing that the proposed reforms to the judicial power could be evaluated only on the basis of Mexico's own political traditions and not on whether this reform was good or bad for socialism. "That is, [it must be judged] within the existence of a government based in the theory of equilibrium and independence of powers, with the object of making possible a government of the majority in Mexico." Lombardo opposed the reform, stating that if it became law, "the judicial power will not be able to operate with all of the independence required." This independence, he continued, could not be dispensed within Mexico's "presidential system," and he echoed the concerns expressed by the Constituent Congress in their opposition to presidential appointment. "Oh poor Court and oh poor country, the day the Court becomes nothing more than a mouthpiece or puppet or producer . . . of the designs of the other powers."[37]

However, as Lombardo and others who opposed the reform quickly discovered, it was much more difficult to argue in favor of this constitutional theory and the need for judicial autonomy in 1928 than it had been just six years earlier, when a similar proposal (also supported by Obregón) had been defeated by Congress. The proposed amendments were most successfully defended by the federal deputy Díaz Soto y Gama, who targeted not just the "reactionary" actions of the justices themselves ("Do you know anything more backwards that more opposes the revolutionary reforms than the spirit of old lawyers?") but also the political tradition that Lombardo was defending.

According to Díaz Soto y Gama, Lombardo was simply defending the liberal jurisprudence of the nineteenth century, and of Ignacio Vallarta in particular. He chided Lombardo, a self-proclaimed Marxist, for his defense of a naïve and "bourgeois" theory of the division of powers. The idea that the Court exercises a regulatory power over the other powers, Díaz Soto y Gama suggested, was exactly what the reactionary interests of landlords and factory owners desired. As a substitute for this older theory, he suggested that the executive branch should be the regulatory power, "obviously oriented by public opinion . . . but never [checked] by the judicial power." If Congress failed to pass this reform, he warned, "the Revolution will have committed suicide and instead of the dictator of one individual, which Lombardo Toledano so fears, of one single revolutionary watched and checked by us, the representatives of the people, elected by popular vote, it will have established . . . the judicial dictatorship of eleven lawyers infected with the jurist's criteria of the roman law."

Behind the ultimate success of the judicial amendments themselves stood the recent history of a Supreme Court that "consistently confirms all sentences that are given against the pueblos . . . expressly violating a categorical article of the Constitution that says that in no case and for no reason will the pueblos that need land be refused the land that they need." During the discussion and to ensure that there were no doubts about the anti-Revolutionary tendencies of the present Supreme Court and its agrarian jurisprudence, Díaz Soto y Gama quoted several documents from a recent agrarian case of April 15, 1928, in which the district court of Puebla nullified a land grant of ejido lands to the town of Temaxcalapa. Although this decision had not yet been heard by the Supreme Court, it was very likely that this sentence was going to be confirmed and, as Díaz Soto y Gama recounted, the American vice consul W. O. Jenkins had stepped in with an offer to resolve the town's need for land. In short, Díaz Soto y Gama concluded, "although it is the President of the Republic who has the constitutional faculty to enforce the revolutionary principles of article 27," judicial opposition to executive power had led to the anomalous situation in which "the foreign hacendado is converted into the arbiter of the agrarian question . . . giving instructions to the towns and district judges and directing agrarian matters, fixing the transactions in order that the ejido lands are given to the communities because the Court does not give them."

W. O. Jenkins was well known as both a foreigner and an owner of large estates. He was, as Díaz Soto y Gama reminded Congress, the epitome of "a capitalist exploiter."[38] The irony of this recent case and its place within a larger pattern of judicial decisions handed down by the Supreme Court were not lost on this particular Congress. The amendment passed, becoming the new law of the land on August 20, 1928. Obregón, however, was not to appoint the justices of a new Court. He was assassinated on July 17, 1928, by a Catholic radical opposed to the anticlerical politics of the Revolutionary government. Instead, that December it would be interim president Emilio Portes Gil who would have the new constitutional responsibility of selecting a new Court that would recognize the new political criteria of Revolutionary agrarian policy.

This successful 1928 amendment to the judicial provisions of the 1917 Constitution "packed" the Court (enlarging its membership to fourteen) and stipulated that amparo cases would now be decided in chambers, with each chamber specializing in a specific field of law (criminal, administrative, and civil). Although the justices retained lifetime tenure, the reform itself had purged the previous membership of the Court and only a few of the old justices were reappointed.[39] These included justices Arturo Cisneros Canto, Jesús Guzmán Vaca, and Salvador Urbina.

Cisneros was a native of the state of Yucatán, where he received his law degree in 1918. He had participated in the radical socialist government of Governor Felipe Carrillo Puerto before becoming a federal deputy and then a Supreme Court justice, in 1927. Guzmán was born in Guanajuato in 1891 and studied law in Morelia, Michoacán. He became a lawyer in 1917 and served in the Jalisco state government of Antonio Valadez Ramírez before his election to the Supreme Court in 1923.[40] Urbina was born in Mexico City, earning his law degree from the National School of Jurisprudence in 1907. Urbina would later become a professor at the National School, teaching courses in political economy and civil procedure. He also served as an agent to the public attorney of the district court of Durango and was subsecretary and then interim secretary of the treasury, among other positions, before his election to the

Supreme Court in 1923. He was to remain an important political figure on the Court throughout the Cárdenas and Avila Camacho periods.[41]

As these brief biographies make clear, these justices were significantly younger than the justices on the first (and second) Revolutionary Court. It is also significant that these three justices had also been arguing for radical new criteria with respect to agrarian jurisprudence and that this minority now formed the majority on the newly created chamber of administrative law. They were joined by two new justices, Daniel Valencia, one year younger than Urbina, and Luis Calderón, probably several years older.[42] Both new justices had served in the federal judicial power previously, in judgeships at the district level.

The new, post-1928 jurisprudence carried forward by Justices Cisneros, Guzmán, Urbina, Valencia, and Calderón was celebrated at the time as the arrival of a truly agrarian Court, for its immediate consequence was to stay thousands of suits against the implementation of both provisional and definitive land grants. Cisneros had been advocating this shift since his appointment to the Court in the fall of 1927. His most radical thesis, which was to be adopted by the new administrative chamber in 1929, was that "the amparo action against administrative resolution is to be stayed [*es improcedente*] when there exists a legal remedy whose effect or result could modify, revoke or reform in whatever form the administrative resolution."[43]

On the basis of this thesis, not only could suits against provisional grants not proceed but even those filing against definitive land grants were instructed by the Court to first exhaust the legal remedies referred to in article 10 of the agrarian law of January 6, 1915, before filing amparo. This article stipulated, "Those who believe their interests to have been damaged by the resolution of the representative of the Executive Power of the Nation may go before the tribunals to deduce their rights within the period of one year, to be counted from the date of said resolution, for past this date, no reclamation will be admitted." However, a favorable judicial resolution only permitted an indemnity in the case of restitution and not the return of granted lands. In the case of dotación this article also allowed that "[i]n the same period of one year those owners of expropriated territory may go before the tribunals, reclaiming the indemnity that should be paid to them."[44]

Although the significance of the new jurisprudence went far beyond the question of agrarian reform, it was the agrarian reform (now conceived as a quasi-judicial process) that was Cisneros's principal focus and motivation.[45] Cisneros also believed that his new jurisprudence in administrative law would swiftly put an end to the backlog problem of the Court, which was diagnosed at the time as one involving amparo against administrative acts and not one of amparo against local judges, as it had been during the last years of the Porfiriato. In effect, Cisneros had simply extended the restriction of a final resolution established for amparo in judicial matters (the initial Porfirian solution to the backlog problem) to the administrative sphere.

Cisneros justified his new jurisprudence in other terms as well. He argued that the previous Court, in continuing to grant amparo, had been ignoring another bundle of rights of equal value, namely the social rights of poor farmers. In other words, the Court's previous jurisprudence had simply privileged one set of rights (those inherited from the 1857 Constitution) over another set of rights (the right, among others, of campesinos, to a piece of land). Consequently, there had been a clear contradiction in the practice of a court that had nonetheless proclaimed itself in favor of the new Revolutionary principles. It was the Court's obligation to more adequately balance these two sets of competing rights. "[O]ne cannot dispute the right of the pueblos to obtain the dotación and restitution of land, nor the faculty of the federal executive to give it to them, because those faculties and right appear plainly in the same Constitution and it would be absurd that a constitutional right and constitutional faculty could be dissolved and nullified by a suit of whatever kind."[46] The amparo in agrarian matters, he argued, had been used and abused with only one purpose in mind: "to buy time, with the manipulative and wrong perspective that in the meantime the Revolutionary government might fall, and with it, its agrarian effort [*obra agraria*]."[47]

We know in hindsight that this new precedent in administrative law failed to fulfill its promise as a truly agrarian jurisprudence and that what seemed expedient, the staying of more than two thousand suits with reference to a practically unused recourse set out in article 10 of the agrarian law of 1915, led to even worse delays in the redistribution of land. As Ignacio Burgoa has explained, landlords responded by filing an ordinary suit (not amparo) before the federal judiciary, citing article 10, but when they did not receive the decision they wanted, there was nothing in the new jurisprudence that prevented them from filing a constitutional suit (amparo) against the circuit court's "definitive" resolution.[48] Thus the Court, having decided to hear these cases, once again became the target for the criticism of agrarians.

Regardless of its ultimate effects, however, this jurisprudence was to be experienced by many commentators as an important transformation of constitutional law that was to have far-reaching consequences for the practice of amparo and the ability of the administration to take an increasingly interventionist role in the sphere of economic life. As such, it aroused a significant number of criticisms and several bitter polemics that portrayed the Court as an accomplice to the exercise of arbitrary power. In response to the Court's initial reversal in an agrarian case filed by Maria Olvera viuda de Figuroa, Eduardo Pallares, the son of the well-known Porfirian jurist Jacinto Pallares, attacked Cisneros and the new jurisprudence of the Court, warning that this new precedent freed a large number of administrative acts from judicial control, with serious consequences for the rights of individuals and the promise of constitutionalism itself.[49] Specifically, he criticized Cisneros's use of analogy in treating an administrative process as identical to the judicial. This was, according to Pallares, a suppression of a distinction critical to the division of powers as traditionally understood. In the judicial process, he explained, "the litigants count with an arsenal of juridical arms that can aid them in defending their rights." This was simply not the case to a significant enough degree in administrative procedures and least of all in agrarian matters. Pallares asked, "[W]ho will control the authority and the resolutions of Mr. President and his Ministers, if the Supreme Court says, 'I wash my hands?'"[50]

Not all commentaries on the new jurisprudence were negative, however. In several articles published between 1929 and 1932, Rodolfo Reyes saw in the Court's new agrarian jurisprudence an example of the increasing "socialization" of the amparo suit (along with the law's recognition of suits filed by the public attorney), which he saw as both a positive and a necessary adjustment to the times. "Indeed, the Constitution of 1917 was affected by the socialization of law; it absolutely recognized it in articles 27 and 123," Reyes argued. However, the Constitution "only went halfway, defining the guarantees in the same way as the individualist one [of 1857] and accepting without change the amparo suit." Because amparo was the "legitimate child of individualism," it was necessary to change it in order to bring it in line with the tendencies of the present. This included the extension of the law to new spheres outside the limits imposed by a traditional conception of liberal individual rights and the division of powers.

Thus it was "a matter of the highest priority" to put the amparo suit in harmony with the law "as it is," which for Reyes clearly included its adaptation to the new agrarian and labor law. He suggested that "the exclusively individual guarantee can be modified and extended as to arrive at those, the so-called social guarantees," that is, the new social rights conceived in their later twentieth-century understanding as human rights. He also suggested that legislation be passed that would simplify and ease the excessive formalism of procedure (a recurring theme in works of this period). But he also warned that it was necessary to avoid the opposite error of turning over "to the discretion of anyone the fate of one's or another's rights, only in lieu of it being simpler—which it is—to resolve arbitrarily some conflict rather than studying and weighing it juridically."[51]

If, as Reyes cautioned, it was a grave error to not look toward the "future," it was equally foolhardy "to depreciate the experiences and successes achieved," especially in relation to amparo, which "has responded in such a way to the reality of our life that . . . even in its perversion it has been useful to us."[52] Having just presided over the incorporation of a new and "socialized" amparo in the republican constitution of Spain, Reyes spoke with considerable authority on the question, despite his persona non grata status among many revolutionaries, a legacy of his collusion with the dictatorship of Victoriano Huerta.[53]

Reyes can be said to represent something of a middle position on the question, and although he approved of the Supreme Court's 1929 jurisprudence he also worried that the impetus to reform the suit could easily be carried too far. Reyes cited the current proposals being advanced by Mexico's attorney general, or *procuraduría general de la república* as well as the thesis of a young Alfonso Noriega.[54] For Noriega, among others, the suit's traditional defense of individual liberty rendered it an anachronism that should be completely overhauled if not abolished.

Indeed, these commentaries indicate how far Revolutionary thinking had traveled from the consensus over amparo in the Constituent Congress of 1916–1917. Already in 1929, writing in response to Pallares's polemic cited above, Andrés Molina Enríquez had argued along these lines:

> That the amparo is dying, as was expressed by Sr. Lic. Don Eduardo Pallares, is a truth as big as a battleship. It has to be. From 1857 to the present, things have changed. Still, in 1857 they had, at least in Mexico, the concept that the State, successor of the old kings, was a capricious and perverse tyrant against which one had to defend oneself at all costs; the social interest, they said then, is in the individual guarantees against the State; but since then the concept of the State has increasingly become one of "*centro director*," and the social interest lies in everyone collaborating with it, reducing the opportunities

> for the rebellious individuals to resist the common action. The present Court has understood this better than the previous ones.[55]

Although Justices Cisneros, Guzmán, Urbina, Valencia, and Calderón would certainly not have shared Molina Enríquez's diagnosis of the situation, they must have realized that their new jurisprudence, a politically motivated strategic retreat, could be perceived as confirming a tendency in the direction outlined by those who felt that amparo should be abolished because of its exclusive focus on rights inherited from the past—an obstacle to Revolutionary social reform. It was probably some consideration of this nature and a desire to counteract a tendency toward the amparo's irrelevance that led Justice Urbina, as part of his annual address of 1929, to propose a constitutional amendment that would "socialize" the suit through "the immediate establishment in our Constitution of social guarantees that, on a par with the individual guarantees, are given the same effect as them through the medium of that suit and are the protective shield of those social groups that in the sphere of economic and political life are distinguished by their common interests, whether they are called labor unions, *ejidatarios*, employer associations or any other group whose special nature or purpose cannot be equated with individuals."

It was, as Urbina recognized, the individualist and "negative" nature of amparo (i.e., proceeding *against* state action) that had led the Court, when it had intervened at all, to intervene in favor of the very interests who were opposing the Revolution's social reforms. For Urbina, his proposal was the only way to bring about "the harmonization of the present system of individual rights, reproduced from the Constitution of 1857 in that of 1917, with the new postulates of the revolution."[56]

However, the next constitutional reform that did come, the 1931 amendment to article 10 of the original agrarian law of January 6, 1915, far from empowering the Court to adjudicate questions of social justice, as the new justices of the administrative chamber might have hoped, instead restricted its powers of oversight, eliminating the use of amparo altogether against violations of the agrarian authorities. This creation of a special agrarian jurisdiction that was purely administrative paid lip service to a rigorous legality that would respect the small property as mandated by the Constitution. However, its ultimate effect was to close the door on the only real guarantee ensuring the legality of these particular administrative acts, to block not only the machinations of large landlords but also the legitimate grievances of small-property owners. The promise that the Court's oversight was to be replaced with an equally vigorous one within the administration itself fell to Mexico's nascent and underdeveloped administrative law.

Those who supported the amendment claimed that the constitutional protection of the small property had simply been used by owners of large estates "for its own interests."[57] It seems likely, however, that for those who supported this particular amendment, the small property was no longer the ultimate goal of the agrarian reform and a clear split within the Revolutionary state was developing between those who continued to sustain the older ideal of a country of small- or medium-sized landholders (implicit in the original constitutionalist project and central to the vision of Calles) and those who believed the future lay in large-scale collectives or "communist" agriculture. As Romana Falcón has shown, the reform was proposed and supported by the Liga Nacional Campesina (LNC) "Ursula Galvan," whose leaders had effectively unified the disparate peasant leagues in one national organization. This political solution to the crisis of implementation was done with an eye to Cárdenas's presidential nomination of 1933 and was carried out with his newfound control of a mobilized peasantry.[58] The reform entered into force in January of 1932 and though it was to be repealed by Miguel Alemán, whose presidential term has been used by some historians to mark the end of the official agrarian reform, it is the most salient example of the degree to which established jurisprudential principles around judicial oversight of the administration, consolidated during the last third of the nineteenth century, had entered into crisis.[59]

It is, of course, Cárdenas who is frequently credited as the first to make real the promises contained in the Revolutionary Constitution, by which is usually meant the social provisions of articles 27 and 123. While he would have been hard-pressed to have successfully redistributed the amounts of land that he did (or in the way he did) if recourse to the judicial branch had not been suspended, this choice can no longer be portrayed as a simple realization of the original intentions of the framers of a new constitution.

It was, after all, also Cárdenas who, as president-elect, introduced that second set of judicial amendments in 1934 that ended any pretense to lifetime tenure and an independent judiciary as a check on executive power.[60] Yet this too had been an important part of the original constitutional vision of 1917. The 1934 reform set new terms for the justices, reducing them to six years in order to correspond with the term of the president, who would appoint the new Court after his election.

Thus it can hardly be denied that this constitutional reform (as well as the two already discussed) represented a clear tendency to weaken judicial autonomy and the constitutional theory of judicial supremacy, and though it may be true that this tendency after 1928 did not lead to a judiciary as politically inconsequential as has sometimes been imagined, it is fairly certain that, as was suggested by contemporaries, the fate of an autonomous judiciary in the immediate post-Revolutionary period remained a prisoner to amparo's nineteenth-century evolution. Although evidence seems to indicate that the Court was not subjectively committed to a defense of the current property regime, its constitutional jurisprudence meant that ultimately its judicial decisions favored those who were.

Conclusion

When historians have sought to assess the important legal changes brought about by the Mexican Revolution they have generally looked to the various Revolutionary plans, to the debates of the Constituent Congress of 1916–1917, and of course, to a comparison of the two constitutional texts, 1857 with that of 1917. Occasionally such accounts have stretched all the way back to include colonial antecedents, but even these have remained bound to an exclusive preoccupation with legislative change. Because these historians have generally ignored the importance of judicial sources, few have even mentioned the fact that one of the obstacles to the implementation of the Constitution's new socioeconomic rights was an amparo-granting Supreme Court that decided hundreds of cases favoring the liberal individual rights of employers and landowners against state and federal governments.

This study began, then, by challenging the tendency in the literature to ignore jurisprudential sources. As we have seen, attention to these sources provides a very different account of the course of Mexican constitutional history. Constitutional change during the Porfiriato, although it mirrored in some respects the political centralization of power that the Porfirian regime is so well known for, did not always serve the narrow class interests of the Porfirian oligarchy, and a robust conception of the institutional scope of amparo existed in the years prior to 1910, a conception that nonetheless excluded political rights to effective suffrage. These changes, and the consolidation of the amparo suit more generally, are important for understanding how the Supreme Court became the obstacle that it did in the years after 1917.

Articles 27 and 123 of the Constitution of 1917 were indeed radical and revolutionary provisions at the time, as even revisionist historians of the Revolution have recognized. But the relevant context for understanding their interpretation in 1917 is the history of what came before, not what came later. What the future would hold could not possibly have been known to the delegates to the Querétaro Constituent Congress or the justices of the first Revolutionary Court. Although many other countries in Europe and Latin America would also seek to address the "social question" in their new constitutions during the interwar period, Mexico's Constitution of 1917 was the first.

Historians of the Revolution have often wondered aloud if the social provisions contained in constitutional articles 27 and 123 really had more than a merely programmatic or symbolic value prior to the six-year term of Lázaro Cárdenas. However, they have rarely mentioned the role of an amparo-granting Supreme Court or the ways in which even the original formulation of articles 27 and 123 was also conditioned by forty years of constitutional jurisprudence. I have argued that many of the deputies to the Constituent Congress were familiar with this tradition of jurisprudence and that the socioeconomic reforms embodied in articles 27 and 123 were initially conceived as additional social limits to liberal individual rights. The Constituent Congress also bolstered the independence of the judicial power through new institutional guarantees designed to guard against executive interference. Changes made to the amparo suit largely confirmed the judge-made changes I have described for the nineteenth century and answered some of the criticisms of the 1908 constitutional amendment to article 102 of the Constitution of 1857 (article 107 of the Constitution of 1917). Secondary legislation that would properly regulate amparo in light of these changes would not come until 1919, but this did not prevent the first Revolutionary Court from admitting and deciding amparos on the basis of past precedent and the older regulatory law as modified by the new constitution. The continuity of amparo and of amparo law, however, allowed those who opposed the Revolutionary principles contained in articles 27 and 123 to successfully file suit in federal courts.

I have also argued that the justices of the Supreme Court, although they decided hundreds of these cases against both labor and agrarian reforms between 1917 and 1934, were not motivated by a hostility toward the new socioeconomic principles themselves. Indeed, a commitment to the legality and correctness of administrative decisions, combined with a conception of their judicial role as impartial arbiters of a legal conflict, put the justices of the third Revolutionary Court at loggerheads with the executive branch over the implementation of the agrarian reform. In the case of labor reform, too, I have argued that the justices did not expand their powers of amparo nor did they creatively reinterpret the substantive meaning of certain liberal individual rights in order to block the implementation of social legislation.

Judicial-executive conflict over the agrarian reform paved the way for the constitutional reforms of 1928 and 1934, long identified by legal scholars as a reversal in the fortunes of an independent judiciary. Indeed, these reforms are a striking counterpoint to the extensive barriers to executive interference put in place by the original Constitution of 1917. However, these constitutional reforms must be analyzed above all in relation to the backlash against the amparo decisions of the Supreme Court. In fact, once the reforms are analyzed, it becomes clear that it is not the weakness but the strength of the federal judiciary that best explains this politicized resolution to the conflict. It is only once a strong and robust tradition of amparo is recognized that we can explain how the Supreme Court became involved in the politically explosive impasse over the implementation of Revolutionary social reform in the first place.

Although it is undeniable that in some areas legal change was accelerated by the Revolution, my study has suggested that the pace of constitutional change during the Mexican Revolution was not as sudden a break as some historical accounts have implied. When jurisprudential sources are also taken into account, it becomes clear that significant constitutional change was characteristic of the periods both before and after the Revolution.

Liberal constitutional principles consolidated prior to 1910 were to enter into crisis in the years after 1920, but these principles were not transformed instantly. In the short run (that is, in the period prior to 1940) most of these changes, especially those that redefined the limits to administrative action in the private sphere, appear to have benefited the working classes. With respect to changes in the Supreme Court's interpretation of constitutional article 123, Narciso Bassols wrote that "as long as the government leaders have been men with clearly defined working class tendencies, then giving the representatives of the government . . . the freedom to decide [labor-capital conflicts] without having to adhere to well-defined norms has been advantageous and just." Whether these legal changes would continue to benefit the interests of this same group in later years was a different story. Already in 1930, Bassols suspected that over time "the representatives of the government" would become more closely aligned with the interests of capital than with the workers.[1] Bassols's prognosis proved remarkably prescient in this regard, not only for the fate of industrial labor but for the *campesinada* as well.

Notes

Introduction

1. Translations of the Constitution of 1917 have been taken from H. N. Branch, "The Mexican Constitution of 1917 Compared with the Constitution of 1857," *Annals of the American Academy of Political and Social Science* 71, supplement (May 1917): 1–116.
2. See, for example, Charles Cumberland, *The Mexican Revolution: The Constitutionalist Years* (Austin: University of Texas Press, 1972), 381–86; Alan Knight, *The Mexican Revolution* (Lincoln: University of Nebraska Press, 1990), 2:515–17; John Womack Jr., "The Mexican Revolution, 1910–1920," in *Mexico Since Independence*, ed. Leslie Bethel (Cambridge: Cambridge University Press, 1991), 179; and Jean Meyer, "Revolution and Reconstruction in the 1920s," in Bethel, *Mexico Since Independence*, 233. In regard to the international dimensions of this problem, see Daniela Spenser, *The Impossible Triangle: Mexico, Soviet Russia, and the United States in the 1920s* (Durham, NC: Duke University Press, 1999); Womack, "Mexican Revolution"; and Friedrich Katz, *The Secret War in Mexico* (Chicago: University of Chicago Press, 1981).
3. Adolfo Gilly, *The Mexican Revolution*, trans. Patrick Camiller (Thetford, UK: Thetford Press, 1983); John M. Hart, *Revolutionary Mexico: The Coming and Process of the Mexican Revolution* (Berkeley: University of California Press, 1987); Ramón E. Ruíz, *The Great Rebellion: Mexico, 1905–1924* (New York: W.W. Norton, 1980).
4. Ruíz, *The Great Rebellion*, 325. See, for example, Pablo Piccato, *The Tyranny of Opinion: Honor in the Construction of the Mexican Public Sphere* (Durham, NC: Duke University Press, 2010), 185. Circuit courts were involved in amparo procedure under legislation passed in 1861. However, they ceased to play a role in amparo proceedings after new legislation was passed in 1869. Hence it is an understandable error made by many unfamiliar with amparo procedure.
5. Peter L. Reich, "Recent Research on the Legal History of Modern Mexico," *Mexican Studies/Estudios mexicanos* 23 (Winter 2007): 192; Mauricio Tenorio Trillo

and Aurora Gómez Galvarriato, *El Porfiriato* (Mexico City: Fondo de Cultura Económica/Centro de Investigación y Docencia Económicas, 2006), 112.

6. Narciso Bassols, *Improcedencia y sobreseimiento en el amparo, según los fallos de la Suprema Corte* (Mexico City: Editorial "Cultura," 1930), 8. As Bassols writes, "En contraste con lo que acontece tratándose de la legislación civil o penal, en las que frente a una inmensa legislación escrita tenemos una mezquina jurisprudencia interpretativa, en el amparo nos encontramos una sencilla, escasa e incompleta ley escrita, junto a una rica y complicada jurisprudencia."
7. Alejandro Mayagoitia, "El concurso científico y artístico del centenario de la independencia o la historia del derecho como ditirambo," *Anuario mexicano de historia del derecho* 13 (2001): 48.
8. An important exception to the rather summary treatment of judicial behavior found in most of this literature is William J. Suarez-Potts, "The Mexican Supreme Court and the *Juntas de Conciliación y Arbitraje*, 1917–1924: The Judicialisation of Labour Relations after the Revolution," *Journal of Latin American Studies* 41, no. 4 (2009): 723–55; cf. Antonio Fernández del Castillo, "Derecho obrero," in *Evolución del derecho mexicano (1912–1942)* (Mexico City: Editorial JUS, 1943), 1:219. For a more extensive discussion of the literature on labor, see chapter 3.
9. Ruíz, *Great Rebellion*, 323, 325–26. For a similar view, also see Timothy J. Henderson, *The Worm in the Wheat: Rosalie Evans and the Agrarian Struggle in the Puebla-Tlaxcala Valley of Mexico, 1906–1927* (Durham, NC: Duke University Press, 1998), 134.
10. Kermit Hall, ed., *The Oxford Guide to United States Supreme Court Decisions* (New York: Oxford University Press, 1999), 162.
11. Aviam Soifer, "The Paradox of Paternalism and Laissez-Faire Constitutionalism: United States Supreme Court, 1888–1921," *Law and History Review* 5, no. 1 (Spring 1987): 250; cf. David E. Bernstein, "*Lochner v. New York:* A Centennial Retrospective," *Washington University Law Quarterly* 83, no. 5 (2005): 1469–527.
12. Hall, *Oxford Guide*, 163.
13. Gertrude Lubbe-Wolff, "Safeguards of Civil and Constitutional Rights: The Debate on the Role of the Reichsgericht," in *German and American Constitutional Thought: Contexts, Interaction, and Historical Realities*, ed. Hermann Wellenreuther (New York: Berg, 1990), 353–72.
14. Peter C. Caldwell, *Popular Sovereignty and the Crisis of German Constitutional Law: The Theory and Practice of Weimar Constitutionalism* (Durham, NC: Duke University Press, 1997), 151.
15. Ibid., 148.
16. For example, Antonio Carrillo Flores, "La Suprema Corte en las reformas sociales de México," *Revista de la Facultad de Derecho de México* 14, no. 55 (1964): 641; Ignacio Burgoa, *El amparo en materia agraria* (Mexico City: Porrúa, 1964), 38;

and Lucio Cabrera, *La Suprema Corte de Justicia durante los años constitucionalistas, 1917–1920* (Mexico City: SCJN, 1995), 1:37–42.

Chapter One

1. For an excellent discussion of these and other issues, see Luis Barrón, *Historias de la Revolución mexicana* (Mexico City: Centro de Investigación y Docenia Económicas/Fondo de Cultura Económica, 2004).
2. Katz, *Secret War*, 5.
3. Héctor Aguilar Camín and Lorenzo Meyer, *In the Shadow of the Mexican Revolution: Contemporary Mexican History, 1910–1989*, trans. Luis Alberto Fierro (Austin: University of Texas Press, 1993), 1; Katz, *Secret War*, 3.
4. Aguilar and Meyer, *In the Shadow of the Mexican Revolution*, 71.
5. The quotation is taken from Arnaldo Córdova, *La ideología de la Revolución mexicana: La formación del nuevo régimen* (Mexico City: Ediciones Era, 1973), 88.
6. Leopoldo Zea, *El postivismo en México* (Mexico City: COLMEX, 1943); Jesús Reyes Heroles, *El liberalismo mexicano*, 3 vols. (Mexico City: UNAM, 1957); Daniel Cosío Villegas, *La Constitución de 1857 y sus críticos*, 4th ed. (Mexico City: Fondo de Cultura Económica, 1998).
7. See, for example, Charles A. Hale, *The Transformation of Liberalism in Late Nineteenth-Century Mexico* (Princeton, NJ: Princeton University Press, 1989).
8. Howard J. Wiarda, *The Soul of Latin America: The Cultural and Political Tradition* (New Haven, CT: Yale University Press, 2001), 164–65.
9. See, for example, Knight, *Mexican Revolution*, 2:476; Womack, "Mexican Revolution," 176; Charles A. Hale, *Emilio Rabasa and the Survival of Porfirian Liberalism* (Stanford, CA: Stanford University Press, 2008).
10. José Barragán Barragán, *Primera ley de amparo de 1861* (Mexico City: Universidad Nacional Autónoma de México, 1987), 80; cf. Oscar Cruz Barney, *Historia del derecho en México* (Mexico City: Oxford University Press, 1999), 604; Richard D. Baker, *Judicial Review in Mexico: A Study of the* Amparo *Suit* (Austin: University of Texas Press, 1971), 27–34.
11. Ignacio L. Vallarta, *El juicio de amparo y el writ of habeas corpus* (Mexico City: Imprenta de Francisco Díaz de Leon, 1881), 39.
12. At this time Mexico's federal judiciary consisted of district courts, circuit courts, and a supreme court, originally made up of eleven *ministros propietarios*, four *supernumarios*, a *fiscal*, and a *procurador general*. With the important exception of the 1861 legislation, circuit courts were not involved in amparo cases.
13. On the "organic laws" that regulated amparo's functioning from 1861 until 1910, see Baker, *Judicial Review in Mexico*, 42–45; José Barragán Barragán, *Proceso de discusión de la ley de amparo de 1869* (Mexico City: UNAM, 1987); José Barragán Barragán, *Proceso de discusión de la ley de amparo de 1882* (Mexico City: UNAM,

1993); Lucio Cabrera, *La Suprema Corte de Justicia: Sus leyes y sus hombres* (Mexico City: SCJN, 1985).

14. Emilio Rabasa, *La Constitución y la dictadura: Estudio sobre la organización política de México*, 3rd ed. (Mexico City: Porrúa, 1956), 45.
15. John Henry Merryman, *The Civil Law Tradition* (Stanford, CA: Stanford University Press, 1969), 30.
16. Francisco Zarco, *Historia del Congreso Extraordinario Constituyente, 1856 y 1857: Extracto de todas sus sesiones y documentos parlamentarios de la época* (Mexico City: Imprenta de I. Cumplido, 1857), 2:499.
17. Ibid., 2:504.
18. As I will explain, these doubts were expressed with reference to the suit's politicization during the 1870s and not primarily in response to the persistence of an older paradigm of legislative supremacy of the kind defended by Ramírez and Hermosillo.
19. Julio García, *Informe rendido a la Suprema Corte de Justicia de la Nación, por su presidente el Sr. Lic. D. Julio García, al terminar el año de 1931* (Mexico City: Antigua Imprenta de Murguía, 1931), 5. The exact number cited by García is 57,792, the vast majority of which related to the application of article 101, fraction I. The relative absence of fractions II and III in the judicial record is undoubtedly a product of the pronounced individualism of the suit as it was interpreted at the time. Even when the federation invaded the jurisdiction of the states, state governments were denied the right to ask for amparo since they were "moral persons" (not real individuals).
20. Secretaría de Justicia e Instrucción Pública, *Memoria que el Secretario de Justicia e Instrucción Pública presenta al Congreso de la Unión, y comprende del 10 de enero de 1878 al 15 de septiembre de 1881* (Mexico City: Tip. Literaria de F. Mata, 1881), 13; Omar Guerrero, *La Secretaría de Justicia y el estado de derecho en México* (Mexico City: UNAM, 1996).
21. This pamphlet is reproduced in Lucio Cabrera, *La Suprema Corte de Justicia a fines del siglo XIX, 1888–1900* (Mexico City: SCJN, 1992), 367. The author also expressed doubts about the ability of the Court to keep up with an increasing backlog of cases, a topic I will discuss later.
22. Rabasa, *La Constitución y la dictadura*, 193.
23. Córdova, *La ideología de la Revolución mexicana*, 216.
24. *El Foro: Periodico de Jurisprudencia y Legislación*, May 16–20, 1874.
25. Vallarta also proposed and defended a constitutional reform passed in 1882 that removed the president of the Court from first in line in the presidential succession.
26. Fernando Vega, *La nueva ley de amparo de garantías individuales: Orgánica de los artículos 101 y 102 de la Constitución* (Mexico City: Imprenta de J. Guzman, 1883), 14.

27. Eduardo Ruíz, *Curso de derecho constitucional y administrativo* (Mexico City: Oficina Tip. de la Secretaría de Fomento, 1888), 1:182.
28. Jacinto Pallares, "Discurso del Sr. Lic. Jacinto Pallares en representación del N. Colegio de Abogados de Mexico," *Revista de legislación y jurisprudencia* 6 (1894): 102.
29. Rabasa, *La Constitución y la dictadura*; also see Cosío, *La Constitución de 1857*, 86–101.
30. This kind of distinction was already insisted on by Isidro Montiel y Duarte in *Legislación comparada: Estudio sobre las garantías individuales* (Mexico City, 1873), 19.
31. Miguel González Avelar, *La Suprema Corte y la política* (Mexico City: UNAM, 1979).
32. On the Vallarta Court in general, see Lucio Cabrera, *La Suprema Corte de Justicia a principios del porfirismo, 1877–1882* (Mexico City: SCJN, 1990).
33. See, for example, Jaime F. Cárdenas García, *Una constitución para la democracia: Propuestas para un nuevo orden constitucional* (Mexico City: UNAM, 1996), 75.
34. François-Xavier Guerra, *México: Del antiguo régimen a la Revolución*, 2 vols. (Mexico City: Fondo de Cultura Económica, 1988); cf. Carlos Bravo Regidor, "Elecciones de gobernadores durante el Porfiriato," in *Las elecciones y el gobierno representativo en México (1810–1910)*, ed. José Antonio Aguilar Rivera (Mexico City: Fondo de Cultura Económica, Consejo Nacional para la Cultura y las Artes, Instituto Federal Electoral, Consejo Nacional de Ciencia y Tecnología, 2010), 257–81.
35. Article 92 of the 1857 Constitution.
36. Rabasa, *La Constitución y la dictadura*, 216.
37. Guerra, *México*, 1:108.
38. Ibid., 2:462–63.
39. Biographical information on the ministros of the Court not found in Guerra has been taken from Suprema Corte de Justicia de la Nación, *Jurisprudencia histórica y otros documentos de la época (1870–1910)* (Mexico City: SCJN, 2005), DVD-ROM; and Roderic A. Camp, *Mexican Political Biographies, 1884–1935* (Austin: University of Texas Press, 1991).
40. Of the fifty-three ministros who served on the Court between 1877 and 1900, twelve, or approximately 23 percent, did not serve out their full six-year term. However, ten of these twelve died while serving on the Court. Of the thirty-one ministros cited by Guerra who served on the Court, thirteen, or 42 percent, were reelected to a second term at least once.
41. Silvestre Moreno Cora mentions Pudenciano Dorantes (1884–1907) in this regard. He also says that Julio Zarate (1897–1906) consistently sided with the ministro público, which frequently represented the interests of the executive. Silvestre Moreno Cora, *Memorias del Ministro Silvestre Moreno Cora* (Mexico City: SCJN, 1998), 583.

42. As far as I know, statistics on split decisions have never been published. However, if we extrapolate from a 20 percent random sample of all amparo cases for the years 1877, 1882, 1887, 1892, and 1897, we get the following numbers: 1877, approximately 30 split decisions; 1882, approximately 726 split decisions; 1887, approximately 85 split decisions; 1892, approximately 191 split decisions; 1897, approximately 304 split decisions.
43. Alejandro Mayagoitia, "Los autores del Dublán y Lozano: Apuntes bibliográficos," in *La legislación mexicana de Manuel Dublán y José María Lozano*, comp. Mario Téllez G. and José López Fontes (Mexico City: Suprema Corte de Justicia, Trib. Superior de Justicia del Estado de México, COLMEX, Escuela Libre, 2004), 56.
44. Cabrera, *La Suprema Corte de Justicia a fines del siglo XIX.*
45. Secretaría de Despacho de Justicia, *Estadística penal y de amparos, 1908: Fuero federal* (Mexico City, 1909). Only articles 2, 3, 9, and 25 were not cited in any case filed before the federal judicial power during this year.
46. Blas José Gutiérrez Flores Alatorre, *Apuntes sobre los fueros y tribunales militares, federales y demas vigentes en la República y sobre las más importantes disposiciones de derecho marítimo, internacional y administrativo relacionados con aquellos* (Mexico City: Imprenta de J. M. Aguilar Ortiz, 1877), 3:125–28. For a historical analysis of the case, see Manuel González Oropeza, "El amparo en negocios judiciales: El caso de Miguel Vega," *Anuario Mexicano de Historia del Derecho* 10 (1998): 385–98.
47. Vallarta, *El juicio de amparo.*
48. Emilio Rabasa, *El artículo 14: Estudio constitucional y El juicio constitucional: Orígenes, teoría y extensión*, 2nd ed. (Mexico City: Editorial Porrúa, 1955), 29.
49. José María Lozano, *Tratado de los derechos del hombre: Estudio del derecho constitucional patrio en lo relativo a los derechos del hombre* (Mexico City: Imprenta del Comercio de Dublán, 1876), 255.
50. Rabasa, *El artículo 14*, 33.
51. Emilio Rabasa, *Derecho constitucional: Conferencias dadas en la Escuela Libre de Derecho en los años de 1927–1928* (Mexico City: Editora de Periódicas, 'La Prensa,' 1961), 187 (emphasis added).
52. Ignacio L. Vallarta, *Cuestiones constitucionales: Votos del C. Ignacio L. Vallarta, presidente de la Suprema Corte de Justicia en los negocios más notables resueltos por este tribunal desde mayo de 1878 a septiembre de 1879* (Mexico City: Imprenta de Francisco Díaz de Leon, 1879), 59–78.
53. Suprema Corte de Justicia, *Amparo promovido por los señores Larrache y Compañía Sucesores contra la sentencia de graduación pronunciada por el juez segundo de lo civil de esta capital el 21 de julio de 1878 en el concurso hipotecario á bienes de don Blas Pereda* (Mexico City: Imprenta del Gobierno en Palacio, 1879), 196.
54. *El Semanario Judicial de la Federación*, segunda época, 10 (May 1886): 791.

55. Archivo Central de la Supreme Corte de Justicia de la Nación, Mexico City, Fondo Ignacio L. Vallarta, Exp. 187, Vallarta to Sr. Don Félix Gilbert, México, August 5, 1885.
56. See, for example, Agustín Rodríguez, *Breve contestación al alegato que el Sr. Lic. Tomás Reyes Retana ha presentado a la Suprema Corte de Justicia para fundar que es de confirmarse la sentencia del sr. juez primero de distrito que ampara a Don Clemente Manuel contra providencias del juez primero de lo civil dictadas en autos que sigue el Sr. D. Eduardo Ebrard contra los Sres F. Donnadieu y Compañía, sobre pesos* (Mexico City: Tipografía T. Gonzalez Sucesores, 1894).
57. Archivo General de la Nación, Mexico City, Archivo Histórico de la Suprema Corte de Justicia de la Nación (Base Digital), Tribunal Pleno, 1893, Juicio de amparo promovido por María Pomposa Dueñas de Zapata Vera contra el Juez de Letras del Partido del Centro de aquel Estado.
58. Archivo Central de la Suprema Corte de Justicia de la Nación, Mexico City, Libros de Actas, Acuerdo Pleno, December 30, 1893. This jurisprudence, it should be noted, resulted in the nullification of aspects of the secondary legislation on amparo passed in 1882.
59. Miguel Mejía, *Errores constitucionales: Las arbitrariedades judiciales y los juicios de amparo; Refutación de los muchos errores que han invadido la jurisprudencia constitucional y exposición de los buenos principios* (Mexico City: Tip. de la Época de Juan B. Acosta, 1886), 5–6.
60. García, *Informe rendido a la Suprema Corte de Justicia de la Nación*, 5.
61. Rabasa, *El artículo 14*, 75.
62. Pallares, “La legislación federal,” 696.
63. Prisciliano Díaz González, “Las jurisprudencias rivales sobre la inteligencia de los artículos 14 y 16 de la Constitución,” *Revista de Legislación y Jurisprudencia* 2 (August–December 1889): 95–111, 461–74.
64. Moreno, *Memorias*, 583–84.
65. “Todos estamos de acuerdo en que la exacta aplicación de la ley es una garantía constitucional aun tratándose de asuntos civiles.” Silvestre Moreno Cora, *Tratado del juicio de amparo conforme a las sentencias de los Tribunales Federales* (Mexico City: Tip. y Lit. “la Europea,” de J. Aguilar Vera, 1902), 631.
66. Suprema Corte de Justicia de la Nación, *El juicio de amparo y el Poder Judicial de la Federación* (Mexico City: SCJN, 1999), 910.
67. The most recent acceptance of Rabasa’s diagnosis is in Hale, *Emilio Rabasa*. For those taking issue with Rabasa’s argument, see Isidro Rojas y Francisco Pascuel García, *El amparo y sus reformas* (Mexico City: Tip. La Compañía Editorial Católica, 1907), 172; Rodolfo Reyes, *Contribución al estudio de la evolución del derecho constitucional en México* (Mexico City: Tip. de la Viuda de F. Díaz de Leon, 1911), 49; Demetrio Sodi, *Progreso realizado en la República desde la Independencia hasta nuestros días en la legislación federal* (Mexico City: Tip. de la Viuda de E Díaz de Leon, 1910).

68. Colegio de Abogados, *Concurso de 1906: Indicación motivada de las reformas que convendría hacer al Código de Procedimientos Federales en el capitulo destinado al juicio de amparo* (Mexico City: Imprenta El Arte Moderno, 1906), 161.
69. Ibid., 210.
70. Ibid., 209, 210.
71. Bolaños, *Discursos que contra el proyecto de ley.*
72. Reyes, *Contribución al estudio*, 49–50.
73. Sodi, *Progreso realizado en la República*, 47.
74. *Diario de los debates del Congreso Constituyente, 1916–1917*, 2nd ed. (Mexico City: Tallares-Gráficos de la Nación, 1960), 1:389.
75. Rabasa, *La Constitución y la dictadura*, 220.
76. Mayagoitia, "El concurso científico y artístico," 30.
77. Robert J. Knowlton, "Tribunales federales y terrenos rurales en el México del siglo XIX: *El Semanario Judicial de la Federación*," *Historia mexicana* 46, no. 1 (1996): 71–98. The disentailment laws should not be confused with federal policies relating to the survey and sale of public lands (*terrenos baldíos*). On the tendency to confuse the two, see Emilio Kouri, "Interpreting the Expropriation of Indian Pueblo Lands in Porfirian Mexico: The Unexamined Legacies of Andrés Molina Enríquez," *Hispanic American Historical Review* 82, no. 1 (2002): 69–117. For an excellent history of the federal policies relating to the survey and sale of public lands, see Robert H. Holden, *Mexico and the Survey of Public Lands: The Management of Modernization* (DeKalb: Northern Illinois University Press, 1994).
78. An observation also made in Moreno, *Tratado del juicio de amparo*, 88–98.
79. Knowlton, "Tribunales federales y terrenos rurales," 78–85.
80. Ibid. However, some of Knowlton's conclusions are limited by the fact that the *Semanario Judicial* does not accurately reflect the totality of amparo cases decided by the Supreme Court. Thus generalizations like "debe señalarse que los casos que tienen que ver con asuntos similares a menudo estaban muy apartados en el tiempo" have more to do with the partial and erratic publishing record of the *Semanario Judicial* than the reality of amparo adjudication during this period.
81. Ibid., 90.
82. Ibid., 93 (emphasis added).
83. Ibid., 96.
84. Moisés González Navarro, *El Porfiriato: La vida social*, vol. 4 of *Historia moderna de México*, ed. Daniel Cosío Villegas (Mexico City: Editorial Hermes, 1957), 236. Also see Katz, *Secret War*, 37.
85. This statistic is based on a 20 percent random sample of the 2,127 total cases filed in this year. For published statistics on the year 1888, see *El Semanario Judicial de la Federación*, segunda época, 14 (January–December 1888). For an interesting example of a case decided in favor of the military authorities, see *El Semanario Judicial de la Federación*, tercera época, 3 (June 1891): 815.

86. *El Semanario Judicial de la Federación*, tercera época, 1 (May 1890): 521.
87. *El Semanario Judicial de la Federación*, cuarta época, 24 (August 1905): 268.
88. *El Semanario Judicial de la Federación*, cuarta época, 28 (September 1906): 352.

Chapter Two

1. Félix F. Palavicini, *¿Cómo y quiénes hicieron la revolución social en México?* (Mexico City: Editorial "Cultura," 1931), 26.
2. Womack, "Mexican Revolution," 130.
3. Paul Garner, *Porfirio Díaz* (London: Pearson Education, 2001), 218.
4. Knight, *Mexican Revolution*, 1:183–84.
5. John Womack Jr., *Zapata and the Mexican Revolution* (New York: Vintage Books, 1970), 70. The one exception was a small paragraph promising a return of lands illegally taken from indigenous communities under the national lands legislation, a provision that caught the attention—as we are told by Womack—of an elected community leader of the town of Anenecuilco, Morelos, Emiliano Zapata.
6. Friedrich Katz, *The Life and Times of Pancho Villa* (Stanford, CA: Stanford University Press, 1998), 123.
7. Womack, "Mexican Revolution," 135–36.
8. Jeffrey Bortz, "The Genesis of the Mexican Labor Relations System: Federal Labor Policy and the Textile Industry, 1925–1940," *Americas* 52, no. 1 (1995): 46. "Only industrialists and government officials participated directly, yet their fear of revolutionary violence led to concessions to workers, otherwise absent from the meeting. The convention reduced the workday from 12 to 10 hours, set a standard wage of 1.25 pesos per day for machine operators and $1.00 for 'peones'—the ubiquitous term for unskilled laborers—and fixed overtime pay at 150% of regular wages. Mill owners acknowledged the principle of dispute arbitration for shop-floor conflict."
9. Jeffrey Bortz, *Revolution Within the Revolution: Cotton Textile Workers and the Mexican Labor Regime, 1910–1923* (Stanford, CA: Stanford University Press, 2008), 97–98. However, to the extent that these proposals gave workers "any voice at all," they were opposed by employers; also see Aguilar and Meyer, *In the Shadow of the Mexican Revolution*, 32.
10. Robert E. Quirk, *The Mexican Revolution, 1914–1915: The Convention of Aguascalientes* (New York: W. W. Norton, 1970), 292.
11. Katz, *Secret War*, 95–115; cf. Knight, *Mexican Revolution*, 1:484–90.
12. Katz, *Secret War*, 120–21; cf. Knight, *Mexican Revolution*, 2:62–103; Michael C. Meyer, *Huerta: A Political Portrait* (Lincoln: University of Nebraska Press, 1972).
13. Luis Barrón, "Porfirian Politics in Revolutionary Mexico: Venustiano Carranza and the Mexican Revolution, 1859–1913" (PhD diss., University of Chicago, 2004),

178. Carranza initially offered the leadership of the 1913 revolution to General Treviño of the federal army.

14. Katz, *Life and Times of Pancho Villa*, 203.
15. Ibid., 213–22.
16. Aguilar and Meyer, *In the Shadow of the Mexican Revolution*, 43–44.
17. Katz, *Secret War*, 123–25; Katz, *Life and Times of Pancho Villa*, chapter 11.
18. Katz, *Life and Times of Pancho Villa*, 123. Another important continuity emphasized by Katz and others was the federal army.
19. Lucio Cabrera, "La Revolución mexicana y la Suprema Corte de Justicia, 1910–1914," in *Diplomacia y revolución: Homenaje a Berta Ulloa*, by Ann Staples et al. (Mexico City: COLMEX, Centro de Estudios Históricos, 2000), 203.
20. Quoted in Cabrera, *La Suprema Corte de Justicia a principios del siglo XX, 1901–1914* (Mexico City: SCJN, 1993), 59–60.
21. Ibid., 67.
22. Ibid., 37. Huerta also offered the leadership of the new government to Carvajal, who, to his credit, refused.
23. Cabrera, "La Revolución mexicana," 205–6.
24. Cabrera, *La Suprema Corte de Justicia a principios del siglo XX*, 79–82.
25. Cabrera, "La Revolución mexicana," 207–8.
26. Ibid., 211.
27. Portions of this decree are reproduced in Gilly, *Mexican Revolution*, 175–77 (emphasis added).
28. Quoted in ibid., 178.
29. Ibid., 173.
30. Knight, *Mexican Revolution*, 2:470.
31. Frank Tannenbaum, *Peace by Revolution: Mexico After 1910* (New York: Columbia University Press, 1929), 166; Knight, *Mexican Revolution*, 2:470–71. Also see Gilly, *Mexican Revolution*, in which the culminating Revolutionary moment is the taking of Mexico City by Zapatistas and Villistas in 1914.
32. Restitution (*restitución*) was designed to ensure the return to indigenous communities of lands that had been taken illegally, either through fraud or by force. If illegality could be proven then no compensation to the expropriated owner was necessary. The latter process, known as dotación (which I have chosen not to translate), was a land grant from the government that was frequently taken from adjacent landowners as an expropriatory act in the name of the public good.
33. Marcelo Blidstein, "Política y caudillismo en el Congreso Constituyente mexicano de 1917," *Mexican Studies/Estudios mexicanos* 16 (Winter 2000): 77.
34. Frank Tannenbaum, *Mexican Agrarian Revolution* (Washington, D.C.: Brookings Institution, 1930), 172–84; Robert E. Quirk, "Liberales y radicales en la Revolución mexicana," *Historia mexicana*, 2, no. 4 (1953): 525.
35. Enrique Florescano, *El nuevo pasado mexicano* (Mexico City: Cal y Arena, 1991).
36. Knight, *Mexican Revolution*, 2:476; Womack, "Mexican Revolution," 176.

37. Cumberland, *Mexican Revolution*, 357.
38. Jorge Sayeg Helú, *El constitucionalismo social mexicano: La integración constitucional de México, 1910–1917* (Mexico City: Cultura y Ciencia Política, 1974); Bertha Ulloa, *La Constitución de 1917*, Historia de la Revolución Mexicana 6 (Mexico City: Colegio de México, 1983), esp. 535.
39. José Ramón Cossío, *La teoría constitucional de la Suprema Corte de Justicia* (Mexico City: Distribuciones Fontamara, 2002), 25, 30–31.
40. Rabasa has highlighted the disagreements in 1856–1857 over judicial supremacy. See Rabasa, *La Constitución y la dictadura*, 45.
41. Cited in Córdova, *La ideología de la Revolución mexicana*, 216. One could also cite the debates of the Revolutionary Convention of Aguascalientes, where amparo (especially its use to nullify illegal elections) was affirmed and defended by none other than Díaz Soto y Gama, the Zapatista ideologue who would later become one of the Court's harshest critics. See *Documentos históricos de la Revolución mexicana*, vol. 25, *La Convención: Debates de las sesiones de la Soberana Convención Revolucionaria, 1914–1915* (Mexico City: Editorial Jus, 1972), 107–12.
42. Linda Arnold, *Política y justicia: La Suprema Corte mexicana, 1824–1855*, trans. José Luis Soberanes Fernández and Julián Bunster (Mexico City: UNAM, Instituto de Investigaciones Jurídicas, 1996), 27–28.
43. For a more complete treatment of the question of the "incompetent by origin" doctrine within the Constituent Congress and beyond, see González, *La Suprema Corte y la política*; on the issue of whether the Court should be able to intervene in relation to the local judiciary, see *Diario de los debates del Congreso Constituyente*, 2:786–95.
44. *Diario de los debates del Congreso Constituyente*, 2:721–22.
45. Ibid., 2:717.
46. Ibid., 2:718.
47. Cossío, *La teoría constitucional*, 32.
48. Jorge Vera Estañol, *Al margen de la Constitución de 1917* (Los Angeles: Wayside Press, 1919), esp. 227–28.
49. Jorge Vera Estañol, "Apuntes de derecho mercantil," 1908, unpublished manuscript, Escuela Libre de Derecho (biblioteca), Mexico City.
50. E. V. Niemeyer Jr., *Revolution at Querétaro: The Mexican Constitutional Convention of 1916–1917* (Austin: University of Texas Press, 1974), 73–74.
51. *Diario de los debates del Congreso Constituyente*, 1:624.
52. Andrés Lira González, "Revolución, derechos sociales y positivismo jurídico en México, 1870–1920," in *Estudios jurídicos en homenaje al maestro Guillermo Flores Margadant* (Mexico City: UNAM, Facultad de Derecho, 1988), 267.
53. *Diario de los debates del Congreso Constituyente*, 1:620.
54. Ibid., 1:628: "[N]o están protegidos por el amparo más que las garantías individuales."
55. Ibid., 1:790.

56. Or as one well-known treatise on amparo put it, "La constitución por una parte proclama los derechos individuales y por otro los limita." Moreno, *Tratado del juicio de amparo*, 47.

57. See, for example, Niemeyer, *Revolution at Querétaro*, 85. Here Niemeyer is forced by the above-cited distinctions to suggest that Múgica was caught in an ideological contradiction when it comes to the debates around article 24. I am suggesting instead that Múgica did not think he was contradicting himself when it came to debates on judicial power or on article 24 and neither did other "radical" delegates.

58. *Diario de los debates del Congreso Constituyente*, 1:675.

59. Ibid., 2:1071.

60. Ibid., 1:977, 1049.

61. Ibid., 1:1028.

62. See, for example, Ignacio Burgoa, *Las garantías individuales*, 34th ed. (Mexico City: Editorial Porrúa, 2001), 719.

63. Lucio Cabrera, *La Suprema Corte de Justicia, la Revolución y el constituyente de 1917, 1914–1917* (Mexico City: SCJN, 1994), 49.

64. *Diario de los debates del Congreso Constituyente*, 1:1049; but cf. 1:1052, "Es pues, un deber de conservacion de humanidad, el que oblige a la Comisión a poner esa restricción a la libertad del trabajo en el artículo 5."

65. Diego Valadés, "Salvador Alvarado, un precursor de la Constitución de 1917," in *Estudios jurídicos en homenaje a don Santiago Barajas Montes de Oca* (Mexico City: UNAM, 1975), 442–43, with reference to Boris Mirkine-Guetzévitch, *Modernas tendencias del derecho constitucional* (Madrid: Editorial Reus, 1934). However, Mexico's precociousness in this regard was recognized by another European, José Miranda, in *Reformas y tendencias constitucionales recientes de la América Latina, 1945–1956* (Mexico City: UNAM, 1957), 232.

66. Vallarta, *El juicio de amparo*, 2.

67. María Becerra González, *Principios de la Constitución mexicana de 1917: Relacionados con el subsuelo, antecedentes doctrinales y legislativos, principios fundamentales contenidos en la Constitución en su versión original y cambios operados después de 1917 en el mismo texto constitucional* (Mexico City: UNAM Coordinación de Humanidades, 1967), 56–58; Alejandra Núñez Luna, "Water Law and the Making of the Mexican State, 1875–1917" (JSD diss., Harvard Law School, 2011); Jeffrey Bortz, "The Legal and Contractual Limits to Private Property Rights in Mexican Industry During the Revolution," in *The Mexican Economy, 1870–1930: Essays on the Economic History of Institutions, Revolution, and Growth*, ed. Jeffrey Bortz and Stephen Haber (Stanford, CA: Stanford University Press, 2002), 267.

68. José María Calderón, *Génesis del presidencialismo* (Mexico City: Ediciones "El Caballito," 1972), 17; Córdova, *La ideología de la Revolución mexicana*, 247.

69. For example, Francisco Múgica; see Adolfo Gilly, *El cardenismo: Una utopía mexicana* (Mexico City: Cal y Arena, 1994), 400–401.
70. See, for example, Otto Kircheimer, "Weimar—and What Then? An Analysis of a Constitution," in *Politics, Law and Social Change: Selected Essays*, ed. Frederic S. Burin and Kurt L. Shell (New York: Columbia University Press, 1969), 33–74.

Chapter Three

1. Héctor Fix-Zamudio, "Ejecutivo federal y el poder judicial," in *El sistema presidencial mexicano: Algunos reflexiónes* (Mexico City: Universidad Nacional Autónoma de México, 1988), 273.
2. Hale, *Transformation of Liberalism*, chapter 4.
3. As a "positivization," to borrow a concept from Mauro Cappelletti, of natural or "higher" law, these articles were also understood at the time to extend to all persons regardless of age, gender, or citizenship and could be enforced as part of a judicial process without violating the prescription that judges should apply the positive law.
4. Suarez-Potts, "Mexican Supreme Court," 735; Suprema Corte de Justicia de la Nación, *Ministros 1917–2004: Semblanzas*, vol. 1 (Mexico: SCJN, 2005).
5. Fundación CONDUMEX—Archivo Venustiano Carranza, Mexico City, fondo XXI, carpeta 26, legajo 2725. González's letter of adhesion to Carranza is dated February 1915.
6. Suprema Corte, *Ministros*, vol. 1.
7. Suarez-Potts, "Mexican Supreme Court," 735–36.
8. Suprema Corte, *Ministros*, vol. 2.
9. *Diccionario histórico y biográfico de la Revolución mexicana*, 8 vols. (Mexico City: Instituto Nacional de Estudios Históricos de la Revolución Mexicana, 1990–1994), vol. 1; cf. Suprema Corte, *Ministros*, vol. 2.
10. Suprema Corte, *Ministros*, vol. 2.
11. *Diccionario histórico y biográfico*, vol. 1.
12. Archivo General de La Nación, Mexico City, Colección Revolución, caja 2, exp. 35, 1–5.
13. *El Universal*, April 7, 1923.
14. *Diario de los Debates*, Cámara de Diputados, Leg. 27, May 26, 1917.
15. "Algunos datos biográficos del Sr. Licenciado Don Victoriano Pimentel," *El Semanario Judicial de la Federación*, quinta época, 12 (October 1923): 392. As the well-known Porfirian jurist Emilio Rabasa wrote in a letter included in the above, Pimentel "[v]ivió abrumado por el trabajo y nunca cuidó de hacer ruido con sus negocios, como lo aconseja la vanidad y la codicia. Lo que puedo asegurar, es que toda su obra es buena, sana, limpia e inteligente."
16. Article 102 of the Constitution of 1857 was modified and expanded, becoming article 107 in the Constitution of 1917. The innovation of an amparo directo

was spelled out in considerable detail in the Constitution itself. Article 107 read, in part,

> Todas las controversias de que habla el artículo 103 [formerly article 101], se seguirán a instancia de la parte agraviada, por medio de procedimientos y formas del orden jurídico que determinará una ley que se ajustará a las bases siguientes: I.- La sentencia será siempre tal, que sólo se ocupe de individuos particulares, limitándose a ampararlos y protegerlos en el caso especial sobre el que verse la queja, sin hacer una declaración general respecto de la ley o acto que la motivare. II.- En los juicios civiles o penales, salvo los casos de la regla IX, el amparo sólo procederá contra las sentencias definitivas respecto de las que no proceda ningún recurso ordinario por virtud del cual puedan ser modificadas o reformadas, siempre que la violación de la ley se cometa, en ellas, o que, cometida durante la secuela del procedimiento, se haya reclamado oportunamente y protestado contra ella por negarse su reparación, y que cuando se haya cometido en primera instancia, se haya alegado en la segunda, por vía de agravio. La Suprema Corte, no obstante esta regla, podrá suplir la deficiencia de la queja en un juicio penal, cuando encuentre que ha habido en contra del quejoso una violación manifiesta de la ley, que lo ha dejado sin defensa o que se le ha juzgado por una ley que no es exactamente aplicable al caso, y que sólo por torpeza no se ha combatido debidamente la violación. III.- En los juicios civiles o penales sólo procederá el amparo contra la violación de las leyes del procedimiento, cuando se afecten las partes substanciales de él y de manera que su infracción deje sin defensa al quejoso. IV.- Cuando el amparo se pida contra la sentencia definitiva, en el juicio civil, sólo procederá, además del caso de la regla anterior, cuando, llenándose los requisitos de la regla segunda, dicha sentencia sea contraria a la letra de la ley aplicable al caso o a su interpretación jurídica, cuando comprenda personas, acciones, excepciones o cosas que no han sido objeto del juicio, o cuando no las comprenda todas por omisión o negativa expresa. Cuando se pida el amparo contra resoluciones no definitivas, según lo dispuesto en la fracción anterior, se observarán estas reglas en lo que fuere conducente. V.- En los juicios penales, la ejecución de la sentencia definitiva contra la que se pide amparo, se suspenderá por la autoridad responsable, a cuyo objeto el quejoso le comunicará, dentro del término que fije la ley y bajo la protesta de decir verdad, la interposición del recurso, acompañando dos copias, una para el expediente y otra que se entregará a la parte contraria. VI.- En juicios civiles, la ejecución de la sentencia definitiva, sólo se suspenderá si el quejoso de fianza de pagar

los daños y perjuicios que la suspensión ocasionare, a menos que la otra parte diese contra fianza para asegurar la reposición de las cosas al estado que guardaban si se concediese el amparo, y pagar los daños y perjuicios consiguientes. En este caso se anunciará la interposición del recurso, como indica la regla anterior. VII.- Cuando se quiera pedir amparo contra una sentencia definitiva, se solicitará de la autoridad responsable copia certificada de las constancias que el quejoso señalare, la que se adicionará con las que indicare la otra parte, dando en ella la misma autoridad responsable, de una manera breve, clara, las razones que justifiquen el acto que se va a reclamar, de las que se dejará nota en los autos. VIII.- Cuando el amparo se pida contra una sentencia definitiva, se interpondrá directamente ante la Suprema Corte, presentándole el escrito con la copia de que se habla en la regla anterior, o remitiéndolo por conducto de la autoridad responsable o del Juez de Distrito del Estado a que pertenezca. La Corte dictará sentencia sin más trámite ni diligencia que el escrito en que se interponga el recurso, el que produzca la otra parte y el Procurador General o el Agente que al afecto designare, y sin comprender otra cuestión legal que la que la queja contenga.

17. Archivo Central de la Suprema Corte de Justicia de la Nación, Mexico City, Actas, Primer Periodo, June 1917, Acuerdo Pleno del Día 6 de junio de 1917.
18. Cabrera, *La Suprema Corte de Justicia: Sus leyes*, 261–71.
19. *El Semanario Judicial de la Federación*, quinta época, 1 (November 1917): 775.
20. Ibid.
21. *El Semanario Judicial de la Federación*, quinta época, 2 (March 1918): 772.
22. Ruíz, *Curso de derecho constitucional y administrativo*, 1:181–82.
23. Vallarta, *Cuestiones constitucionales*, 1:404–5.
24. Ibid.
25. See, for example, *El Semanario Judicial de la Federación*, segunda época, 10 (January 1886): 331; segunda época, 10 (June 1886): 876; segunda época, 14 (February 1888): 307, 321, 350; segunda época, 14 (April 1888): 739; tercera época, 3 (June 1891): 813; cuarta época, 28 (September 1906): 440.
26. Indeed, these changes brought with them the first continuous elaboration of modern administrative law in Mexico, according to Gustavo R. Velasco, "Derecho administrativo," in *Evolución del derecho mexicano*, 1:50.
27. Tribunal del Tercero Circuito, *Sentencia pronunciada por el Tercer Tribunal de Circuito: En autos seguidos por la extinguida Comunidad del Villa Unión contra los denunciantes del predio "Siqueros" publicada por el Lic. A Yriarte* (Mazatlán, Mexico: Tip. y Casa Editorial de M. Retes, 1897), with reference to a sentence of August 11, 1896.

28. *Diario de los debates del Congreso Constituyente*, 1:1040.
29. Ignacio Marván Laborde, "De instituciones y caudillos: Las relaciones entre la Cámara de Diputados de la XXVIII Legislatura y el Presidente Carranza," *Historia mexicana* 51, no. 2 (2001): 261–323; Jeffrey Weldon, "Political Sources of *Presidencialismo* in Mexico," in *Presidentialism and Democracy in Latin America*, ed. Scott Mainwaring and Mathew Soberg Shugart (New York: Cambridge University Press, 1997), 225–58.
30. Cámara de Diputados, *Dictamen de la primera comisión especial para el estudio y presentación de leyes reglamentarias que consulta una iniciativa de ley del trabajo* (Mexico City: Imprenta de la Cámara de Diputados, 1917), 2–3.
31. Archivo Central de la Suprema Corte de Justicia de la Nación, Mexico City, Versiónes Taquigráficas, pleno, agosto y septiembre 1918, August 31, 1918.
32. Ibid. (emphasis added).
33. Archivo Central de la Suprema Corte de Justicia de la Nación, Mexico City, Versiónes Taquigráficas, pleno, enero y marzo 1918, January 12, 1918.
34. Ibid.
35. Ibid.
36. For an excellent analysis of these changes, see Suarez-Potts, "Mexican Supreme Court," 736–37, 744–46.
37. Jeffrey Bortz, "'Without Any More Law Than Their Own Caprice': Cotton Textile Workers and the Challenge to Factory Authority During the Mexican Revolution," *International Review of Social History* 42 (1997): 256.
38. Ibid.
39. This is especially true for Veracruz, which has traditionally been singled out for the large number of "labor disturbances" that took place during the Revolution and was one of the first to pass regulatory legislation for article 123, which "was in some respects more favorable to labor than was the constitution." Marjorie Ruth Clark, *Organized Labor in Mexico* (Chapel Hill: University of North Carolina Press, 1934), 53–54. Also see Aurora Gómez, "Impact of Revolution: Business and Labor in the Mexican Textile Industry, Orizaba, Veracruz, 1900–1930" (PhD diss., Harvard University, 2000); and Jeffrey Bortz, "The Revolution, the Labour Regime and Conditions of Work in the Cotton Textile Industry in Mexico, 1910–1927," *Journal of Latin American Studies* 32, no. 3 (2000): 671–703.
40. Barry Carr, *El movimiento obrero y la política en México, 1910–1929* (Mexico City: Ediciones Era, 1981), 82–91.
41. John M. Hart, *Anarchism and the Mexican Working Class, 1860–1931* (Austin: University of Texas Press, 1978).
42. María del Carmen Collado Herrera, *Empresarios y políticos, entre la Restauración y la Revolución, 1920–1924* (Mexico City: Instituto Nacional de Estudios Históricos de la Revolución Mexicana, 1996).
43. Jorge Basurto, *El proletariado industrial en México* (Mexico City: UNAM, 1975), 221–24. Although the CROM was the most important union at the national level,

it was certainly not the only one. During the early 1920s, for example, the CGT (Confederación General de Trabajadores) was an important competitor. On communist influence, see Daniela Spenser, *Stumbling Its Way Through Mexico: The Early Years of the Communist International*, trans. Peter Gellert (Tuscaloosa: University of Alabama Press, 2011).

44. Kevin Middlebrook, *The Paradox of Revolution* (Baltimore: Johns Hopkins University Press, 1995), 62.
45. Jeffrey Bortz, "Authority Re-seated: Control Struggles in the Textile Industry During the Mexican Revolution," *Labor History* 44, no. 2 (2003): 171–88.
46. Bortz, "Legal and Contractual Limits," 270.
47. "[N]o cabe recurso alguno"; *El Semanario Judicial de la Federación*, quinta época, 3 (December 1918): 1337.
48. Middlebrook, *Paradox of Revolution*, 56.
49. For one of the first of such resolutions, see *El Semanario Judicial de la Federación*, quinta época, 2 (March 1918): 772. For a decision against a Michoacan law, see *El Semanario Judicial de la Federación*, quinta época, 3 (September 1918): 728. It is important to remember that such declarations did not have *erga omnes* effect (i.e., the effect of applying to all). However, just because they did not have erga omnes effect does not mean that they did not present a barrier to implementation that concerned legislative and executive officials alike.
50. Ernest Gruening, *Mexico and Its Heritage* (New York: D. Century, 1928), 365; "Solicitud de la Unión Minera Mexicana," Archivo Central de la Suprema Corte de Justicia de la Nación, Mexico City, Versiónes Taquigráficas, pleno, April 2, 1922; *El Universal*, February 21, March 11, 1922. However, the same newspaper also blamed Congress for not passing regulatory legislation. See *El Universal*, February 21, 1922.
51. *Diario de los Debates*, Cámara de Diputados, Leg. 29, October 7, 1921.
52. Lucio Cabrera, *La Suprema Corte de Justicia durante el gobierno del Presidente Obregón* (Mexico City: SCJN, 1996), 439.
53. Suarez-Potts, "Mexican Supreme Court," 744–45.
54. *El Universal*, February 21, 1922.
55. For a useful discussion of the importance of the new collective contracts, see Bortz, "Genesis of the Mexican Labor Relations System."
56. Eduardo Delhumeau, *La administración de justicia: Nuevo sistema de enjuiciamiento civil* (Mexico City: Imprenta "la editor nacional," 1917).
57. Weldon, "Political Sources of *Presidencialismo*," 231; *El Demócrata*, July 25, 1923. Other justices supported by the PNC majority of Congress included Leopoldo A. Estrada and Gustavo Vicencio.
58. *Diccionario histórico y biográfico*, vol. 1.
59. Enrique Plasencia de la Parra, *Personajes y escenarios de la rebelión Delahuertista, 1923–24* (Mexico City: Instituto de Investigaciónes Históricas, UNAM, 1998).

60. Archivo Central de la Suprema Corte de Justicia de la Nación, Mexico City, Actas, Acuerdo Pleno, January 12, 1924.
61. Ibid., January 18, 1924.
62. Gustavo Vicencio, also retained from the earlier (second) Court, also expressed reservations about granting new powers to the labor boards.
63. Lucio Cabrera, *La Suprema Corte de Justicia durante el gobierno del Presidente Plutarco Elías Calles* (Mexico City: SCJN, 1997), 262–65; Suarez-Potts, "Mexican Supreme Court," 749.
64. Cabrera, *La Suprema Corte de Justicia durante el gobierno Calles*, 262.
65. The Court went as far as to declare unconstitutional state codes that mandated otherwise. See especially Archivo Central de la Suprema Corte de Justicia de la Nación, Mexico City, Actas, Versiónes Taquigráficas, segunda sala, agosto II 1933, August 30, 1933.
66. *El Semanario Judicial de la Federación*, quinta época, 17 (November 1925): 1195; quinta época, 14 (April 1925): 960.
67. Clark, *Organized Labor*, 248–51.
68. Max Weber, *Economy and Society: An Outline of Interpretative Sociology*, ed. and trans. Guenther Roth and Claus Wittich (Berkeley: University of California Press, 1978), 2:980.
69. Benito Javier Pérez Verdía, *El problema obrero: Patronal conferencia sustentada por el Lic. Benito Javier Pérez Verdía, bajo los auspicios del Centro Patronal de Jalisco, de la Confederación Patronal de Jalisco, de la Confederación Patronal de la Rep. Mexicana* (Guadalajara, Mexico: 1936), 5.
70. The chief justice, for his part, had aided the escape from Mexico City of one of the more important generals implicated in the rebellion in December. See Plasencia, *Personajes y escenarios*, 221.
71. Cabrera, *La Suprema Corte de Justicia durante el gobierno Calles*, 308.

Chapter Four

1. Luis Cabrera, "La reforma del artículo 10 de la ley de 6 de enero," in *La Revolución es la Revolución* (Mexico City: CEN, 1985), 213.
2. Archivo Central de la Suprema Corte de Justicia de la Nación, Mexico City, Versiónes Taquigráficas, pleno, noviembre 1928, November 14, 1928.
3. For the complete text, see Cabrera, "La reforma del artículo 10," 207–8.
4. *El Semanario Judicial de la Federación*, quinta época, 3 (August 1918): 542.
5. Archivo Central de la Suprema Corte de Justicia de la Nación, Mexico City, Versiónes Taquigráficas, pleno, enero a marzo 1918, March 11, 1918.
6. Lucio Mendieta y Núñez, *El problema agrario de México y la ley federal de reforma agraria*, 10th ed. (Mexico City: Porrúa, 1981), 214. For a copy of the 1918 draft law

and a request for the reactivation of the project, see Cámara de Senadores, puntos constitucionales, Leg. XXVIII, Libro 451, p. 1018.

7. *Diccionario histórico y biográfico*, vol. 5.
8. For the early jurisprudence on suspension, see *El Semanario Judicial de la Federación*, quinta época, 1 (October 1917): 400; quinta época, 2 (February 1918): 305; quinta época, 3 (July 1918): 72.
9. *El Semanario Judicial de la Federación*, quinta época, 2 (April 1918): 1050.
10. *El Semanario Judicial de la Federación*, primera época, 1 (March 1871): 297; segunda época, 6 (September 1883): 419; segunda época, 7 (September 1884): 575; segunda época, 11 (August 1886): 230; segunda época, 12 (March 1887): 268; segunda época, 15 (September 1888): 334; tercera época, 3 (March 1891): 244; segunda época, 16 (March 1889): 504. For a case that was not decided in favor of the complainant, see *El Semanario Judicial de la Federación*, segunda época, 14 (March 1888): 512.
11. Archivo Central de la Suprema Corte de Justicia de la Nación, Mexico City, Versiónes Taquigráficas, pleno, enero a marzo 1918, January 31, 1918.
12. Archivo General de la Nación, Mexico City, Obregón/Calles, 818-E-28, Anexo I, "Sobre criterio de la corte en revocacion de sentencias administrativas por parte de las mismas autoridades," December 28, 1921.
13. Javier Garciadiego Dantán, personal communication, May 2004.
14. Paul Friedrich, *Agrarian Revolt in a Mexican Village: 1920–1926* (Chicago: University of Chicago Press, 1977), 96–97.
15. Burgoa, *El amparo en materia agraria*, 38.
16. Mendieta y Núñez, *El problema agrario*, 215–16.
17. *El Semanario Judicial de la Federación*, quinta época, 10 (June 1922): 1099.
18. Ibid.
19. Ibid.
20. *El Semanario Judicial de la Federación*, quinta época, 18 (June 1926): 1243.
21. Ibid.
22. *El Semanario Judicial de la Federación*, quinta época, 19 (August 1926): 325. According to Ignacio Burgoa, this new jurisprudence was to be confirmed in numerous sentences, including amparos filed by Elena Sesma Vda. de Ruiz, Carlos Arellano Valle, Valentina Azcue de Bernot, and Amalia Ramírez de Muñoz; see Burgoa, *El amparo en materia agraria*, 37.
23. *El Semanario Judicial de la Federación*, quinta época, 19 (July 1926): 215.
24. Aguilar and Meyer, *In the Shadow of the Mexican Revolution*, 114–15; Jesús Silva Herzog, *El agrarismo mexicano y la reforma agraria: Exposición y crítica*, 2nd ed. (Mexico City: Fondo de Cultura Económica, 1964), 322.
25. Jürgen Buchenau, *Plutarco Elías Calles and the Mexican Revolution* (Lanham, MD: Rowman and Littlefield, 2007), 122–23; Jürgen Buchenau, *The Last Caudillo:*

Alvaro Obregón and the Mexican Revolution (Hoboken, NJ: Wiley-Blackwell, 2007), 119–21.

26. Quoted in Burgoa, *El amparo en materia agraria*, 42–44.
27. *El Semanario Judicial de la Federación*, quinta época, 18 (June 1926): 1243.
28. Bassols, *La nueva ley agraria* (Mexico City, 1927), 82: "Es indiscutible que la garantía del artículo 14 que exige un juicio previo para la pérdida de la propiedad, está satisfecha, porque la interpretación de los conceptos de ese artículo que hablan de tribunales, hemos visto que no puede llevarnos a la conclusion, exagerada, de que solamente habrá tribunales cuando se trate de autoridades dependientes del Poder Judicial."
29. Archivo General de la Nación, Mexico City, Obregón/Calles, 104-S-32, Vicencio to Calles, April 17, 1925.
30. Archivo General de la Nación, Mexico City, Obregón/Calles, 241-P.3.-P.-1, Padilla to Calles, June 9, 1926.
31. *El Globo*, January 28, 1925; *Diario de los Debates*, Cámara de Diputados, Leg. 33, December 2, 1931. The exact number given by *El Globo* and based on numbers released by the Supreme Court was 1,462.
32. Cabrera, "La reforma del artículo 10," 219.
33. Bassols, *La nueva ley agraria*, 72–73.
34. Mireya Toto, *El amparo de la pequeña propiedad agraria* (Mexico City: Editorial Grijalbo, 1986), 37.
35. Archivo Central de la Suprema Corte de Justicia de la Nación, Mexico City, Versiónes Taquigráficas, pleno, noviembre 1928, November 14, 1928.
36. Cossío, *La teoría constitucional*, 22–32.
37. *Diario de los Debates*, Cámara de Diputados, Leg. 32, May 18, 1928.
38. Ibid.
39. As Justice Padilla put it to a friend in 1929, "[D]iferencias de criterio con el actual régimen me hicieron salir de la Suprema Corte." Fideicomiso Archivos Plutarco Elías Calles y Fernando Torreblanca, Mexico City, Exp. 9, Inv. 4285, PADILLA, Manuel, July 8, 1929, Padilla to lic. D. Ismael Palafox. On the one hand, Díaz Soto y Gama asserted that Padilla was an important exception to his criticisms of the reactionary nature of the Supreme Court (both had served the convention government); on the other hand, Padilla was not considered a *callista*.
40. Suprema Corte, *Ministros*, 1:141, 343.
41. Suprema Corte, *Ministros*, 2:719; Camp, *Mexican Political Biographies*, 216; Gruening, *Mexico and Its Heritage*, 504; Antonio Carrillo Flores, *La defensa jurídica de los particulares frente a la administración en México* (Mexico City: Porrúa Hermanos, 1939), 339.
42. Suprema Corte, *Ministros*, 2:729, 1:83. Biographical information on Calderón is quite limited. We do not know when he was born or what his experience was prior to becoming a district judge.

43. Archivo Central de la Suprema Corte de Justicia de la Nación, Mexico City, Versiónes Taquigráficas, pleno, octubre 1928, October 10, 1928.
44. Manuel Fabila, *Cinco siglos de legislación agraria en México* (Mexico City: Los Talleres de Industrial Gráfica, 1943), 274.
45. "La resolución provisional tiene el mismo efecto que un fallo dictado en primera instancia y que tiene apelación . . . hay contienda, porque hay uno que demanda, uno que contesta, uno que ataca y otro que se defiende, entonces, por que no aplicar los principios generales admitidos por la ley de amparo," as these were applied to judicial authorities. Quoted in Cabrera, *La Suprema Corte de Justicia durante el gobierno Calles*, 67.
46. Arturo Cisneros Canto, *¿El juicio de garantías solo procede contra actos definitivos?* (Mexico City, 1931), 20.
47. Ibid., 13.
48. Burgoa, *El amparo en materia agraria*, 40.
49. *El Universal*, January 26, 1929.
50. *El Universal*, February 5, 1929.
51. *El Universal*, August 3, 1932.
52. *El Universal*, September 6, 1934.
53. Reyes had joined the cabinet of Gen. Victoriano Huerta after the coup against Madero, which had been led by his father, Bernardo Reyes.
54. Alfonso Noriega, "El juicio de amparo" (Tesis, Universidad Nacional de México, 1930), cited in Rodolfo Reyes, *La defensa constitucional: Recursos de inconstitucionalidad y amparo* (Madrid: Espasa-Calpe, 1934), 274.
55. *El Universal*, May 4, 1929, quoted in Cabrera, *La Suprema Corte de Justicia durante los gobiernos de Portes Gil, Ortiz Rubio y Abelardo L. Rodríguez*, 2:187–88.
56. Lucio Cabrera, *La Suprema Corte de Justicia durante los gobiernos de Portes Gil, Ortíz Rubio y Abelardo L. Rodríguez* (Mexico City: SCJN, 1998), 2:208–9.
57. Marte R. Gomez, quoted in Dana Markiewicz, *The Mexican Revolution and the Limits of the Agrarian Reform, 1915–1946* (Boulder, CO: Lynne Rienner, 1993), 157.
58. Cited in Toto, *El amparo de la pequeña propiedad agraria*, 50–51.
59. Markiewicz, *Mexican Revolution*, 163.
60. Also in 1934, changes to article 10 of the original agrarian law made in 1931 (barring the use of amparo) were incorporated into the text of article 27 itself.

Conclusion

1. Quoted in Cabrera, *La Suprema Corte de Justicia durante el gobierno Calles*, 308.

Selected Bibliography

Archival Sources (Mexico City)

Archivo Central de la Suprema Corte de Justicia de la Nación
Archivo General de la Nación
Archivo Histórico del Senado
Fideicomiso Archivos Plutarco Elías Calles y Fernando Torreblanca
Fundación CONDUMEX—Archivo Venustiano Carranza

Published Primary Sources

Aguirre Berlanga, Manuel. *Reformas a la Constitución.* 1917.

Aponte López, Francisco. *Memorial dirigido a la Suprema Corte de Justicia de la Nación por la H. Legislatura del Estado . . . los amparos promovidos contra la erección en pueblos libres de algunas haciendas y ranchos de este estado.* 1918.

Badillo, Roman. *Trabajo presentado por el Sr. Lic. Roman Badillo, del Sindicato de Abogados del DF en el congreso jurídico que se celebró en el anfiteatro Bolívar de la escuela nacional preparatoria los días veinte a treinta de septiembre de 1932: Conciliación del derecho de propiedad privada con la aspiración agrarista.* 1932.

Barra, Lauro. *Exposición que eleva a la Suprema Corte de Justicia el Lic. Lauro Barra, apoderado de los vecinos del Presidio o Villa Unión en el amparo que han pedido los vecinos de Siqueiros ante el Juez de Distrito de Sinaloa, contra una resolución de la Secretaría de Fomento.* Mexico City: Impr. y Litografía "La Europea" de F. Camacho, 1896.

Bassols, Narciso. *Improcedencia y sobreseimiento en el amparo, según los fallos de la Suprema Corte.* Mexico City: Editorial "Cultura," 1930.

———. *La nueva ley agraria.* Mexico City, 1927.

———. *Obras.* Mexico City: Fond de Cultura Económica, 1964.

Bautista, José María. *El octavo magistrado de la Suprema Corte de los Estados-Unidos Mexicanos, da cuenta al pueblo, de su conducta, en el desempeño de su encargo.* Mexico City: Imprenta de Ignacio Escalante, 1883.

Bolaños Cacho, Miguel. *Los derechos del hombre: Integridad personal y real.* Vol. 1. Mexico City: A. Carranza e Hijos, 1909.

———. *Discursos que contra el proyecto de ley que restringe el juicio de amparo al adicionar el artículo 102 de la Constitución federal, pronuncio el Senador Lic. Miguel Bolaños Cacho en la Cámara de Senadores del Congreso de la Unión, en la sesión del día 13 de junio de 1908.* Mexico City: Imprenta Benito Juárez, 1908.

Branch, H. N. "The Mexican Constitution of 1917 Compared with the Constitution of 1857." *Annals of the American Academy of Political and Social Science* 71, supplement (May 1917): 1–116.

Cabrera, Luis. *La Revolución es la Revolución.* Mexico City: CEN, 1985.

Cámara de Diputados. *Diario de los debates de la H. Cámara de Diputados, 1916–1994.* Mexico City: LV Legislatura, Comité de Biblioteca, 1994.

———. *Dictamen de la primera comisión especial para el estudio y presentación de leyes reglamentarias que consulta una iniciativa de ley del trabajo.* Mexico City: Imprenta de la Cámara de Diputados, 1917.

Casale, Miguel A. *Alegato presentado por el súbdito italiano Miguel A. Casale en el juicio de amparo promovido ante el juzgado de distrito en el Estado Libre y Soberano de Coahuila de Zaragoza contra ciertos actos del jefe político de Sierra Mojada, C. Juan Castillon.* 1898.

Cisneros Canto, Arturo. *¿El juicio de garantías solo procede contra actos definitivos?* Mexico City, 1931.

Colegio de Abogados. *Concurso de 1906: Indicación motivada de las reformas que convendría hacer al Código de Procedimientos Federales en el capítulo destinado al juicio de amparo.* Mexico City: Imprenta El Arte Moderno, 1906.

Compañía Minera Naica. *El amparo promovido por la Compañía Minera de Naica, SA: Opiniones de varios prominentes abogados del foro mexicano sobre este asunto.* 1920.

Concursos sobre temas de derecho industrial. Mexico City, 1928.

Cortés, Francisco. *El juicio de amparo al alcance de todos.* Mexico City: Imprenta y Fototipia de la Sec. de Fomento, 1908.

Cue, José de. *Las garantías constitucionales en Tabasco: Ataque a la propiedad con fuerza armada, o violación flagrante del artículo 16 de la Constitución; Documentos justificativos; El juez de distrito no suspendió el acto reclamado.* San Juan Bautista, Tabasco, Mexico: Tip. Mercantile de F. Gallegos, 1896.

Delhumeau, Eduardo. *La administración de justicia: Nuevo sistema de enjuiciamiento civil.* Mexico City: Imprenta "la editor nacional," 1917.

Dominguez, Guillermo. *Asunto "El Herrero," "La Casita," y "Las Demasías": Cuestiones constitucionales en el incidente de ejecución de la ejecutoria de la Suprema*

Corte de Justicia Federal. Guaymas, Mexico: Impr. y Encuadernación de E. Gaxiola, 1897.

Dublán, Manuel, and José María Lozano. *Legislación mexicana ó colección completa de las disposiciones legislativas expedidas desde la Independencia de la República*. 41 vols. Mexico City, 1876–1910.

Espinosa, Gonzalo. *Principios de derecho constitucional: Garantías individuales*. Mexico City: Tip. José del Rivero, 1905.

Flores, Benito. *El juicio de amparo en el derecho mexicano: Estudio leído en inglés por el Lic. Benito Flores, magistrado de la Suprema Corte de Justicia en la República Mexicana, en la reunión celebrada el 6 de julio de 1921 por the Texas Bar Association, en la ciudad de San Antonio, Texas*. Mexico City: Antigua Imprenta de Murguía, 1921.

García, Julio. *Informe rendido a la Suprema Corte de Justicia de la Nación, por su presidente el Sr. Lic. D. Julio García, al terminar el año de 1931*. Mexico City: Antigua Imprenta de Murguía, 1931.

Gil, Agustín. *Exposición relativa a un juicio de amparo promovido contra procedimientos de la jefatura de Hacienda de Guanajuato y ejecutoria de la Suprema Corte de Justicia declarando que el uso de la facultad coactive no viola garantía alguna constitucional por el Lic. Agustín Gil: Oficial encargado del Ramo de Nacionalización en la misma jefatura de hacienda*. 1890.

Gruening, Ernest. *Mexico and Its Heritage*. New York: D. Century, 1928.

Gutiérrez Flores Alatorre, Blas José. *Apuntes sobre los fueros y tribunales militares, federales y demás vigentes en la República y sobre las más importantes disposiciones de derecho marítimo, internacional y administrativo relacionados con aquellos*. 4 vols. Mexico City: Imprenta de J. M. Aguilar Ortiz, 1876–1878.

Horcasitas, Andrés. *Sentencia del Tribunal de Circuito de México: Condenando a los denunciantes del pueblo de San Miguel Chaputepec, Estanislao Castellanos y socios a prestar la caución judicatum solvi en favor de los opositores a la demanda de baldíos: Le procede un prólogo del Lic. D. Prisciliano María Díaz González, abogado de los opositores*. Mexico City: Impr. Popular de J. J. Terrazas, 1892.

Horcasitas, Andrés, and Ignacio L. Vallarta. *Dictámenes de los Señores Licenciados Andrés Horcasitas e Ignacio L. Vallarta el primero sobre el denuncio de la Cuenca del Jaramillo y cuestiones relativas, y el segundo acerca de la invasión de las minas nombradas Guadalupe y el Rosario, del Mineral de Pachuca*. Mexico City: Oficina Tip. de la Secretaria de Fomento, 1889.

Lozano, José María. *Estudio del derecho constitucional patrio en lo relativo a los derechos del hombre*. 3rd ed. Mexico City: Porrúa, 1980.

Mariscal, Ignacio. "Algunas reflexiones sobre el juicio de amparo." In *El pensamiento jurídico mexicano*, edited by Daniel Moreno, 879–96. Mexico City: Porrúa, 1966.

Mejía, Miguel. *Errores constitucionales: Las arbitrariedades judiciales y los juicios de amparo; Refutación de los muchos errores que han invadido la jurisprudencia constitucional y exposición de los buenos principios.* Mexico City: Tip. de la Época de Juan B. Acosta, 1886.

Montiel y Duarte, Isidro. *Legislación comparada: Estudio sobre las garantías individuales.* Mexico City, 1873.

Moreno Cora, Silvestre. *Memorias del Ministro Silvestre Moreno Cora.* Mexico City: SCJN, 1998.

———. *Tratado del juicio de amparo conforme a las sentencias de los tribunales federales.* Mexico City: Tip. y Lit. "la Europea," de J. Aguilar Vera, 1902.

Novoa, Eduardo. *Estudio presentado a la Suprema Corte de Justicia de la Nación, por el Señor Magistrado D. Eduardo Novoa: Al discutirse el amparo que el Ayuntamiento de Ixtapalapa promovió contra el fallo dictado con aplicación inexacta de la ley, por la Cuarta Sala del Tribunal Superior de Justicia del Distrito Federal en un juicio seguido entre el sindico del mismo ayuntamiento y el C. Antonio Elorriaga.* Mexico City: Secretaría de Fomento, 1898.

Palavicini, Félix F. *¿Cómo y quiénes hicieron la revolución social en México?* Mexico City: Editorial "Cultura," 1931.

Pallares, Eduardo. *La jurisprudencia de la Suprema Corte de Justicia: Colección debidamente clasificada y extractada de las sentencias de más importancia, pronunciadas por la Suprema Corte de Justicia de la Nación, a partir del mes de junio de 1917 hasta junio de 1919.* Mexico City: Herrero Hermanos Sucesores, 1921.

Pallares, Jacinto. *Legislación federal complementaria del derecho civil mexicano.* Mexico City, 1897.

———. *El poder judicial o tratado completo de la organización, competencia y procedimientos de los tribunales de la República Mexicana.* Mexico City: Imprenta del Comercio de Navor Chávez, 1874.

Peña, Lic. J. de J. *La institución de amparo: Estudio constitucional.* C. Victoria "El Ramo de Olivo," Ciudad Victoria, Mexico, 1908.

Pérez Verdía, Benito Javier. *El problema obrero: Patronal conferencia sustentada por el Lic. Benito Javier Pérez Verdía, bajo los auspicios del Centro Patronal de Jalisco, de la Confederación Patronal de Jalisco, de la Confederación Patronal de la Rep. Mexicana.* Guadalajara, Mexico, 1936.

Portugal, Jesús J. *Amparo. Lic. Jesús J. Portugal, patrono de los vecinos del pueblo de Apipilulco, contra actos del Juzgado de Distrito del Estado de Guerrero y Supremo Tribunal del Tercer Circuito: Bienes nacionalizados.* Mexico City: Impr. de A. L. Parra, 1905.

Proyecto de reformas a la Constitución federal para la reorganización del poder judicial. 1922.

Rabasa, Emilio. *El artículo 14: Estudio constitucional y El juicio constitucional: Orígenes, teoría y extensión.* 2nd ed. Mexico City: Editorial Porrúa, 1955.

———. *La Constitución y la dictadura: Estudio sobre la organización política de México.* 3rd ed. Mexico City: Porrúa, 1956.

Reyes, Audomaro. *Alegato presentado ante la Corte Suprema de Justicia de la Nación por Tabasco Electrical & Improvement Company en el juicio de amparo que ha seguido contra el Ayuntamiento de San Juan Bautista de Tabasco y el ejecutivo del estado de este último nombre por la destrucción de su línea de alumbrado eléctrico.* Mexico City, 1901.

Reyes, Rodolfo. *Contribución al estudio de la evolución del derecho constitucional en México.* Mexico City: Tip. de la Viuda de F. Diaz de León, 1911.

———. *La defensa constitucional: Recursos de inconstitucionalidad y amparo.* Madrid: Espasa-Calpe, 1934.

Rodríguez, Ramón. *Derecho constitucional escrito para servir de texto a los alumnos del Colegio Militar.* 1875.

Rojas, Isidro. *Consulta que el Ministerio de Fomento, Colonización e Industria hace a aquella respetable corporación por acuerdo del señor presidente de la República: ¿Pueden declararse denunciables los criaderos de carbón de piedra en todas sus variedades, así como los manantiales de petróleo, existan o no en terrenos de propiedad particular?; Voto razonado del académico Lic. Isidro Rojas.* Mexico City: Antigua Casa Editorial "José María Mellado," 1905.

Rojas, Isidro, and Francisco Pascuel García. *El amparo y sus reformas.* Mexico City: Tip. La Compañía Editorial Católica, 1907.

Romero, Félix. *Informe presentado a la Corte Suprema de Justicia de la Nación el 30 de mayo de 1908 por su presidente el Lic. don Félix Romero.* Mexico City: Antigua Imprenta de Murguía, 1908.

Ruíz, Eduardo. *Curso de derecho constitucional y administrativo.* 2 vols. Mexico City: Oficina Tip. de la Secretaría de Fomento, 1888.

Sánchez, Indalecio. *Amparo en negocios judiciales: Estudio de derecho constitucional y civil por el Lic. Indalecio Sánchez Gavito.* Mexico City: Impr. de Francisco Díaz de León, 1879.

Secretaría de Despacho de Justicia. *Estadística penal y de amparos, 1908: Fuero federal.* Mexico City, 1909.

Secretaría de Industria, Comercio y Trabajo. *Junta federal de conciliación y arbitraje: Reglamento de las juntas federales de conciliación y arbitraje.* 1928.

Secretaría de Justicia e Instrucción Pública. *Memoria que el Secretario de Justicia e Instrucción Pública presenta al Congreso de la Unión, y comprende del 10 de enero de 1878 al 15 de septiembre de 1881.* Mexico City: Tip. Literaria de F. Mata, 1881.

———. *Memoria que el Secretario de Justicia e Instrucción Pública Lic. Joaquín Baranda presenta al Congreso de la Unión en cumplimiento del precepto constitucional: Comprende desde el 10 de abril de 1887 hasta el 30 de noviembre de 1888.* Mexico City: Imp. de Gobierno Federal, en el Ex-Arzobispado, 1889.

———. *Memoria que el Secretario de Justicia e Instrucción Pública Lic. Justino Fernández presenta al Congreso de la Unión: Comprende en el ramo de justicia desde el 10 de diciembre de 1896 hasta el 31 de diciembre de 1900, y en el de instrucción pública.* Mexico City: Antigua Imp. J. F. Jeans, 1902.

Sierra, Justo. *Obras completas.* 15 vols. Mexico City: UNAM, 1948–1993.

Sodi, Demetrio. *Procedimientos federales.* Mexico City: Imprenta y Fototipia de la Secretaría de Fomento, 1912.

———. *Progreso realizado en la República desde la Independencia hasta nuestros días en la legislación federal.* Mexico City: Tip de la Viuda de E. Díaz de León, 1910.

Suprema Corte de Justicia. *Amparo promovido por los señores Larrache y Compañía Sucesores contra la sentencia de graduación pronunciada por el juez segundo de lo civil de esta capital el 21 de julio de 1878 en el concurso hipotecario á bienes de don Blas Pereda.* Mexico City: Imprenta del Gobierno en Palacio, 1879.

Tejada, C. Trejo Lerdo de. *Derecho administrativo mexicano (legislación civil federal): Su formación y desarrollo de 1810–1910.* Mexico City: Tip de la Viuda de F. Díaz de León, 1911.

Tribunal del Tercero Circuito. *Sentencia pronunciada por el Tercer Tribunal de Circuito: En autos seguidos por la extinguida Comunidad de Villa Unión contra los denunciantes del predio "Siqueiros" publicada por el Lic. A. Yriarte.* Mazatlán, Mexico: Tip. y Casa Editorial de M. Retes, 1897.

Vallarta, Ignacio L. *Cuestiones constitucionales: Votos del c. Ignacio L. Vallarta, presidente de la Suprema Corte de Justicia en los negocios más notables resueltos por este tribunal desde mayo de 1878 a septiembre de 1879.* Mexico City: Imprenta de Francisco Díaz de León, 1879.

———. *El juicio de amparo y el writ of habeas corpus.* Mexico City: Imprenta de Francisco Díaz de León, 1881.

Vega, Fernando. *La nueva ley de amparo de garantías individuales: Orgánica de los artículos 101 y 102 de la Constitución.* Mexico City: Imprenta de J. Guzman, 1883.

Vera Estañol, Jorge. *Al margen de la Constitución de 1917.* Los Angeles: Wayside Press, 1919.

Viesca, Francisco. *Fundamentos morales del derecho público.* Mexico City: Tip de la Viuda de F. Díaz de León, 1911.

Zarco, Francisco. *Historia del Congreso Extraordinario Constituyente, 1856 y 1857: Extracto de todas sus sesiones y documentos parlamentarios de la época.* 2 vols. Mexico City: Imprenta de I. Cumplido, 1857.

Periodicals (Mexico City)

Anuario de Legislación y Jurisprudencia

Excelsiór

El Foro: Órgano de la Orden Mexicana de Abogados

El Foro: Periódico de Jurisprudencia y Legislación

El País

Revista de Legislación y Jurisprudencia

El Semanario Judicial de la Federación

El Universal

Secondary Sources

Aguilar Camín, Héctor, and Lorenzo Meyer. *In the Shadow of the Mexican Revolution: Contemporary Mexican History, 1910–1989*. Translated by Luis Alberto Fierro. Austin: University of Texas Press, 1993.

Agustine-Adams, Kif. "Marriage and *Mestizaje*, Chinese and Mexican: Constitutional Interpretation and Resistance in Sonora, 1921–1935." *Law and History Review* 29, no. 2 (May 2011): 419–63.

Arenal Fenochio, Jaime del. "Derecho de juristas: Un tema ignorado por la historiografía jurídica mexicana." *Revista de Investigaciones Jurídicas* 15 (1991): 145–66.

Arnold, Linda. *Política y justicia: La Suprema Corte mexicana, 1824–1855*. Translated by José Luis Soberanes Fernández and Julián Bunster. Mexico City: UNAM, Instituto de Investigaciones Jurídicas, 1996.

Avila Espinosa, Felipe. *El problema agrario a fines del Porfiriato y en los comienzos de la Revolución*. Vol. 5, *La justicia durante el Porfiriato y la Revolución, 1898–1914*. Mexico City: Suprema Corte de Justicia de la Nación, 2010.

Baker, Richard D. *Judicial Review in Mexico: A Study of the* Amparo *Suit*. Austin: University of Texas Press, 1971.

Barragán Barragán, José. *Proceso de discusión de la ley de amparo de 1869*. Mexico City: UNAM, 1987.

———. *Proceso de discusión de la ley de amparo de 1882*. Mexico City: UNAM, 1993.

Barrón, Luis. *Carranza: El último reformista porfiriano*. Mexico City: Tusquets Editores México, 2009.

———. *Historias de la Revolución mexicana*. Mexico City: Centro de Investigación y Docenia Económicas/Fondo de Cultura Económica, 2004.

Basurto, Jorge. *El proletariado industrial en México*. Mexico City: UNAM, 1975.

Beatty, Edward. *Institutions and Investment: The Political Basis of Industrialization in Mexico Before 1911*. Stanford, CA: Stanford University Press, 2001.

Becerra González, María. *Principios de la Constitución mexicana de 1917: Relacionados con el subsuelo, antecedentes doctrinales y legislativos, principios fundamentales contenidos en la Constitución en su versión original y cambios operados después de 1917 en el mismo texto constitucional*. Mexico City: UNAM Coordinación de Humanidades, 1967.

Benjamin, Thomas, and Mark Wasserman, eds. *Provinces of the Revolution: Essays on Regional Mexican History, 1910–1929*. Albuquerque: University of New Mexico Press, 1990.

Blidstein, Marcelo. "Política y caudillismo en el Congreso Constituyente mexicano de 1917." *Mexican Studies/Estudios mexicanos* 16 (Winter 2000): 39–78.

Bortz, Jeffrey. "The Genesis of the Mexican Labor Relations System: Federal Labor Policy and the Textile Industry, 1925–1940." *Americas* 52, no. 1 (1995): 43–67.

———. "The Legal and Contractual Limits to Private Property Rights in Mexican Industry During the Revolution." In *The Mexican Economy, 1870–1930: Essays on the Economic History of Institutions, Revolution, and Growth*, edited by

Jeffrey Bortz and Stephen Haber, 255–88. Stanford, CA: Stanford University Press, 2002.

———. "The Revolution, the Labour Regime and Conditions of Work in the Cotton Textile Industry in Mexico, 1910–1927." *Journal of Latin American Studies* 32, no. 3 (2000): 671–703.

———. *Revolution Within the Revolution: Cotton Textile Workers and the Mexican Labor Regime, 1910–1923*. Stanford, CA: Stanford University Press, 2008.

Boyer, Christopher. *Becoming Campesinos: Politics, Identity, and Agrarian Struggle in Postrevolutionary Michoacán, 1920–1935*. Stanford, CA: Stanford University Press, 2003.

Bravo Regidor, Carlos. "Elecciones de gobernadores durante el Porfiriato." In *Las elecciones y el gobierno representativo en México (1810–1910)*, edited by José Antonio Aguilar Rivera, 257–81. Mexico City: Fondo de Cultura Económica, Consejo Nacional para la Cultura y las Artes, Instituto Federal Electoral, Consejo Nacional de Ciencia y Tecnología, 2010.

Brown, Jonathan C. *Oil and Revolution in Mexico*. Berkeley: University of California Press, 1993.

Buchenau, Jürgen. *The Last Caudillo: Alvaro Obregón and the Mexican Revolution*. Hoboken, NJ: Wiley-Blackwell, 2007.

———. *Plutarco Elías Calles and the Mexican Revolution*. Lanham, MD: Rowman and Littlefield, 2007.

Buchenau, Jürgen, and William H. Beazley, eds. *State Governors in the Mexican Revolution, 1910–1952*. Lanham, MD: Rowman and Littlefield, 2009.

Buffington, Robert. *Criminal and Citizen in Modern Mexico*. Lincoln: University of Nebraska Press, 2000.

Burgoa, Ignacio. *El amparo en materia agraria*. Mexico City: Porrúa, 1964.

———. *Las garantías individuales*. 34th ed. Mexico City: Editorial Porrúa, 2001.

———. *El juicio de amparo*. 10th ed. Mexico City: Editorial Porrúa, 1975.

Cabrera, Lucio. *El poder judicial federal mexicano y el constituyente de 1917*. Mexico City: UNAM, 1968.

———. "La Revolución mexicana y la Suprema Corte de Justicia, 1910–1914." In *Diplomacia y revolución: Homenaje a Berta Ulloa*, by Ann Staples et al., 195–212. Mexico City: COLMEX, Centro de Estudios Históricos, 2000.

———. *La Suprema Corte de Justicia durante el fortalecimiento del porfirismo, 1882–1888*. Mexico City: SCJN, 1991.

———. *La Suprema Corte de Justicia durante el gobierno del Presidente Obregón*. Mexico City: SCJN, 1996.

———. *La Suprema Corte de Justicia durante el gobierno del Presidente Plutarco Elías Calles*. Mexico City: SCJN, 1997.

———. *La Suprema Corte de Justicia durante los años constitucionalistas, 1917–1920*. 2 vols. Mexico City: SCJN, 1995.

———. *La Suprema Corte de Justicia durante los gobiernos de Portes Gil, Ortíz Rubio y Abelardo L. Rodríguez*. 2 vols. Mexico City: SCJN, 1998.

———. *La Suprema Corte de Justicia a fines del siglo XIX, 1888–1900.* Mexico City: SCJN, 1992.

———. *La Suprema Corte de Justicia: Sus leyes y sus hombres.* Mexico City: SCJN, 1985.

———. *La Suprema Corte de Justicia a principios del porfirismo, 1877–1882.* Mexico City: SCJN, 1990.

———. *La Suprema Corte de Justicia a principios del siglo XX, 1901–1914.* Mexico City: SCJN, 1993.

———.*La Suprema Corte de Justicia en la República restaurada, 1867–1876.* Mexico City: SCJN, 1989.

———. *La Suprema Corte de Justicia, la Revolución y el constituyente de 1917, 1914–1917.* Mexico City: SCJN, 1994.

Calderón, José María. *Génesis del presidencialismo.* Mexico City: Ediciones "El Caballito," 1972.

Caldwell, Peter C. *Popular Sovereignty and the Crisis of German Constitutional Law: The Theory and Practice of Weimar Constitutionalism.* Durham, NC: Duke University Press, 1997.

Cappelletti, Mauro. *El control judicial de la constitucionalidad de las leyes en el derecho comparado.* Mexico City: UNAM, 1966.

Cappelletti, Mauro, and John Clarke Adams. "Judicial Review of Legislation: European Antecedents and Adaptations." *Harvard Law Review* 79 (March 1966): 1207–24.

Cárdenas García, Jaime F. *Una constitución para la democracia: Propuestas para un nuevo orden constitucional.* Mexico City: UNAM, 1996.

Carpizo, Jorge. *La Constitución mexicana de 1917.* Mexico City: UNAM, Coordinación de Humanidades, 1969.

Carr, Barry. *Marxism and Communism in Twentieth-Century Mexico.* Lincoln: University of Nebraska Press, 1992.

———. *El movimiento obrero y la política en México, 1910–1929.* Mexico City: Ediciones Era, 1981.

Carrillo Flores, Antonio. *La defensa jurídica de los particulares frente a la administración en México.* Mexico City: Porrúa Hermanos, 1939.

———. "La Suprema Corte en las reformas sociales de México." *Revista de la Facultad de Derecho de México* 14, no. 55 (1964): 639–62.

Casar Pérez, María Amparo, and Ignacio Marván, eds. *Gobernar sin mayoría: México 1867–1997.* México: Taurus/CIDE, 2002.

Chavez Padrón, Martha. "Breve historia de los tribunales agrarios en México, al través del artículo 27 de la Constitución federal." *Revista de la Facultad de Derecho de México* 42 (1992): 37–67.

Clark, Marjorie Ruth. *Organized Labor in Mexico.* Chapel Hill: University of North Carolina Press, 1934.

Cockcroft, James D. *Precursores intelectuales de la Revolución mexicana, 1900–1913.* Mexico City: Siglo Veintiuno, 1980.

Collado Herrera, María del Carmen. *Empresarios y políticos, entre la restauración y la*

Revolución, 1920–1924. Mexico City: Instituto Nacional de Estudios Históricos de la Revolución Mexicana, 1996.

Córdova, Arnaldo. *La ideología de la Revolución mexicana: La formación del nuevo régimen*. Mexico City: Ediciones Era, 1973.

Cosío Villegas, Daniel. *La Constitución de 1857 y sus críticos*. 4th ed. Mexico City: Fondo de Cultura Económica, 1998.

———. *Historia moderna de México*. Vol. 8, *El Porfiriato. Vida política interior. Primera parte*. Mexico City: Hermes, 1988.

———. *Historia moderna de México*. Vol. 9, *El Porfiriato. Vida política interior. Segunda parte*. Mexico City: Hermes, 1993.

Cossío, José Ramón. *La teoría constitucional de la Suprema Corte de Justicia*. Mexico City: Distribuciones Fontamara, 2002.

Cruz Barney, Oscar. *Historia del derecho en México*. Mexico City: Oxford University Press, 1999.

Cueva, Mario de la. "La Constitución política." In *México, 50 años de revolución*. Vol. 3, *La política*. Mexico City: Fondo de Cultura Económica, 1961.

Cumberland, Charles. *The Mexican Revolution: The Constitutionalist Years*. Austin: University of Texas Press, 1972.

———. *Derecho mexicano del trabajo*. Mexico City: Porrúa Hermanos, 1938.

Domingo, Pilar. "Judicial Independence: The Politics of the Supreme Court in Mexico." *Journal of Latin American Studies* 32 (2000): 151–75.

Dulles, John W. F. *Yesterday in Mexico: A Chronicle of the Revolution, 1919–1936*. Austin: University of Texas Press, 1961.

Dunn, John. *The Cunning of Unreason: Making Sense of Politics*. New York: Basic Books, 2001.

Fabila, Manuel. *Cinco siglos de legislación agraria en México*. Mexico City: Los Talleres de Industrial Gráfica, 1943.

Fallaw, Ben. *Cárdenas Compromised: The Failure of Reform in Postrevolutionary Yucatán*. Durham, NC: Duke University Press, 2001.

Fix-Zamudio, Héctor. "Ejecutivo federal y el poder judicial." In *El sistema presidencial mexicano: Algunos reflexiónes*, 269–364. Mexico City: Universidad Nacional Autónoma de México, 1988.

———. *Ensayos sobre el derecho de amparo*. Mexico City: UNAM, 1993.

Florescano, Enrique. *El nuevo pasado mexicano*. Mexico City: Cal y Arena, 1991.

Friedrich, Paul. *Agrarian Revolt in a Mexican Village, 1920–1926*. Chicago: University of Chicago Press, 1977.

Garner, Paul. *Porfirio Díaz*. London: Pearson Education, 2001.

Gilly, Adolfo. *El cardenismo: Una utopía mexicana*. Mexico City: Cal y Arena, 1994.

———. *The Mexican Revolution*. Translated by Patrick Camiller. Thetford, UK: Thetford Press, 1983.

Gledhill. John. *Casi Nada: A Study of Agrarian Reform in the Homeland of Cárdenismo*. Albany: Institute for Mesoamerican Studies, State University of New York, 1991.

Gómez, Aurora. "Impact of Revolution: Business and Labor in the Mexican Textile Industry, Orizaba, Veracruz, 1900–1930." PhD diss., Harvard University, 2000.

González Avelar, Miguel. *La Suprema Corte y la política*. Mexico City: UNAM, 1979.

Guerra, François-Xavier. *México: Del antiguo régimen a la Revolución*. 2 vols. Mexico City: Fondo de Cultura Económica, 1988.

Guerrero, Omar. *La Secretaría de Justicia y el estado de derecho en México*. Mexico City: UNAM, 1996.

Haber, Stephen, Armando Razo, and Noel Maurer. *The Politics of Property Rights: Political Instability, Credible Commitments, and Economic Growth in Mexico, 1876–1929*. New York: Cambridge University Press, 2003.

Hale, Charles A. *Emilio Rabasa and the Survival of Porfirian Liberalism*. Stanford, CA: Stanford University Press, 2008.

———. *The Transformation of Liberalism in Late Nineteenth-Century Mexico*. Princeton, NJ: Princeton University Press, 1989.

Hart, John M. *Anarchism and the Mexican Working Class, 1860–1931*. Austin: University of Texas Press, 1978.

———. *Revolutionary Mexico: The Coming and Process of the Mexican Revolution*. Berkeley: University of California Press, 1987.

Henderson, Timothy J. *The Worm in the Wheat: Rosalie Evans and the Agrarian Struggle in the Puebla-Tlaxcala Valley of Mexico, 1906–1927*. Durham, NC: Duke University Press, 1998.

Holden, Robert H. *Mexico and the Survey of Public Lands: The Management of Modernization*. DeKalb: Northern Illinois University Press, 1994.

James, T. M. "Derecho constitucional y el juicio de amparo durante el Porfiriato." In *De Cádiz al siglo XXI: Doscientos años de constitucionalismo en México e Hispanoamérica (1812–2012)*, edited by Adriana Luna, Pablo Mijangos, and Rafael Rojas, 253–90. Mexico City: Taurus/CIDE, 2012.

———. "Liberal Jurisprudence, Labor Tribunals and Mexico's Supreme Court, 1917–1924." *Law and History Review* 27, no. 1 (2009): 87–112.

———. *Revolución social e interpretación constitucional: La Suprema Corte y las reformas sociales revolucionarias, 1916–1934*. Mexico City: SCJN, 2010.

Joseph, G. M. *Revolution from Without: Yucatan, Mexico, and the United States, 1880–1924*. New York: Cambridge University Press, 1982.

Katz, Friedrich. "The Liberal Republic and the Porfiriato." In *Mexico Since Independence*, edited by Leslie Bethel, 49–124. Cambridge: Cambridge University Press, 1991.

———. *The Life and Times of Pancho Villa*. Stanford, CA: Stanford University Press, 1998.

———. *The Secret War in Mexico*. Chicago: University of Chicago Press, 1981.

Kircheimer, Otto. *Politics, Law and Social Change*. New York: Colombia University Press, 1969.

Knight, Alan. "Cardensimo: Juggernaut or Jalopy?" *Journal of Latin American Studies* 26, no. 1 (February 1994): 73–107.

———. *The Mexican Revolution.* 2 vols. Lincoln: University of Nebraska Press, 1990.

Knowlton, Robert J. "Tribunales federales y terrenos rurales en el México del siglo XIX: *El Semanario Judicial de la Federación.*" *Historia mexicana* 46, no. 1 (1996): 71–98.

Kouri, Emilio. "Interpreting the Expropriation of Indian Pueblo Lands in Porfirian Mexico: The Unexamined Legacies of Andrés Molina Enríquez." *Hispanic American Historical Review* 82, no. 1 (2002): 69–117.

———. *A Pueblo Divided: Business, Property, and Community in Papantla, Mexico.* Stanford, CA: Stanford University Press, 2004.

Kroeber, Clifton B. *Man, Land, and Water: Mexico's Farmlands Irrigation Policies, 1885–1911.* Berkeley: University of California Press, 1984.

Kuntz Ficker, Sandra. *La Reforma Agraria durante los años veinte en los expedientes de la Suprema Corte de Justicia de la Nación.* Mexico City: SCJN, 2012.

Lira González, Andrés. *El amparo colonial y el juicio de amparo mexicano.* Mexico City: Fondo de Cultura Económica, 1972.

———. *Comunidades indígenas frente a la ciudad de México: Tenochitlán y Tlatelolco, sus pueblos y barrios, 1812–1919.* Mexico City: El Colegio de México/Colegio de Michoacán, 1983.

———. "Los derechos del hombre, las personas morales y el juicio de amparo en los albores del siglo XX." In *El mundo del derecho: Aproximaciones a la cultura jurídica novohispana y mexicana (siglos XIX y XX)*, edited by Jaime del Arenal and Elisa Speckman Guerra, 111–71. Mexico City: Universidad Nacional Autónoma de México, Instituto de Investigaciones Históricas/Escuela Libre de Derecho/Porrúa, 2009.

———. "Revolución, derechos sociales y positivismo jurídico en México, 1870–1920." In *Estudios jurídicos en homenaje al maestro Guillermo Flores Margadant*, 259–72. Mexico City: UNAM, Facultad de Derecho, 1988.

Lomnitz, Claudio. "Modes of Citizenship in Mexico." *Public Culture* 11, no. 1 (1999): 269–93.

Lubbe-Wolff, Gertrude. "Safeguards of Civil and Constitutional Rights: The Debate on the Role of the Reichsgericht." In *German and American Constitutional Thought: Contexts, Interaction, and Historical Realities*, edited by Hermann Wellenreuther, 353–72. New York: Berg, 1990.

Markiewicz, Dana. *The Mexican Revolution and the Limits of the Agrarian Reform, 1915–1946.* Boulder, CO: Lynne Rienner, 1993.

Márquez Colín, Graciela. *De contribuyentes y recaudadores: Una mirada a los impuestos a través de los expedientes del archivo histórico de la Suprema Corte de Justicia de la Nación.* Vol. 4, *La justicia durante el Porfiriato y la Revolución, 1898–1914.* Mexico City: Suprema Corte de Justicia de la Nación, 2010.

Marshall, T. H. *Citizenship and Social Class.* Cambridge: Cambridge University Press, 1950.

Marván Laborde, Ignacio. "De instituciones y caudillos: Las relaciones entre la Cámara de Diputados de la XXVIII Legislatura y el Presidente Carranza." *Historia mexicana* 51, no. 2 (2001): 261–323.

Matute, Alvaro. *La carrera del caudillo. Historia de la Revolución mexicana,* 8. Mexico City: Colegio de México, 1980.

Mayagoitia, Alejandro. "El concurso científico y artístico del centenario de la independencia o la historia del derecho como ditirambo." *Anuario mexicano de historia del derecho* 13 (2001): 29–111.

Medin, Tzvi. *Ideología y praxis política de Lázaro Cárdenas.* Mexico City: Siglo Veintiuno Editores, 1997.

Mendieta y Núñez, Lucio. *El problema agrario de México y la ley federal de reforma agraria.* 10th ed. Mexico City: Porrúa, 1968.

———. *El sistema agrario constitucional: Explicación e interpretación del artículo 27 de la Constitución política de los Estados Unidos Mexicanos en sus preceptos agrarios.* Mexico City: Librería de Porrúa Hermanos, 1940.

Merryman, John Henry. *The Civil Law Tradition.* Stanford, CA: Stanford University Press, 1969.

Meyer, Jean. *La révolution mexicaine, 1910–1940.* Paris: Calmann-Lévy, 1973.

Meyer, Jean, Enrique Krauze, and Cayetano Reyes. *Estado y sociedad con Calles. Historia de la Revolución mexicana,* 11. Mexico City: Colmex, 1981.

Meyer, Michael C. *Huerta: A Political Portrait.* Lincoln: University of Nebraska Press, 1972.

Meyers, William K. *Forge of Progress, Crucible of Revolt. The Origins of the Mexican Revolution in La Comarca Lagunera, 1880–1911.* Albuquerque: University of New Mexico Press, 1994.

———. "Politics, Vested Rights, and Economic Growth in Porfirian Mexico: The Company Tlahualilo in the Comarca Lagunera, 1885–1911." *Hispanic American Historical Review* 57, no. 2 (1977): 425–54.

Middlebrook, Kevin. *The Paradox of Revolution.* Baltimore: Johns Hopkins University Press, 1995.

Mijangos y González, Pablo. *El nuevo pasado jurídico mexicano.* Madrid: Editorial Dykinson, 2011.

Miranda, José. *Reformas y tendencias constitucionales recientes de la América Latina, 1945–1956.* Mexico City: UNAM, 1957.

Mirkine-Guetzévitch, Boris. *Modernas tendencias del derecho constitucional.* Madrid: Editorial Reus, 1934.

Mirow, M. C. *Latin American Law: A History of Private Law and Institutions in Spanish America.* Austin: University of Texas Press, 2004.

———. "*Marbury* in Mexico: Judicial Review's Precocious Southern Migration." *Hastings Constitutional Law Quarterly* 35 (2007): 41–117.

Moreno, Daniel. *El Congreso Constituyente de 1916–17.* Mexico City: UNAM-Coordinación de Humanidades, 1967.

Niemeyer, E. V., Jr. *Revolution at Querétaro: The Mexican Constitutional Convention of 1916–1917.* Austin: University of Texas Press, 1974.

Núñez Luna, Alejandra. "Water Law and the Making of the Mexican State, 1875–1917." JSD diss., Harvard Law School, 2011.

Orantes, Romeo Leon. *El juicio de amparo.* Mexico City: Editorial Superación, 1941.

Parada Gay, Francisco. *Breve reseña histórica de la Suprema Corte de Justicia de la Nación.* Mexico City: Antigua Imprenta de Murguía, 1929.

Piccato, Pablo. *City of Suspects: Crime in Mexico City, 1900–1931.* Durham, NC: Duke University Press, 2001.

———. *Congreso y revolución.* Mexico City: Instituto Nacional de Estudios Históricos de la Revolución Mexicana, 1991.

———. *The Tyranny of Opinion: Honor in the Construction of the Mexican Public Sphere.* Durham, NC: Duke University Press, 2010.

Plasencia de la Parra, Enrique. *Personajes y escenarios de la rebelión Delahuertista, 1923–24.* Mexico City: Instituto de Investigaciones Históricas, UNAM, 1998.

Quirk, Robert E. "Liberales y radicales en la Revolución mexicana." *Historia mexicana* 2, no. 4 (1953): 503–28.

———. *The Mexican Revolution, 1914–1915: The Convention of Aguascalientes.* New York: W.W. Norton, 1970.

Ramírez Rancaño, Mario. *Los amparos entre el Ejército Federal: 1898–1914.* Vol. 1, *La justicia durante el Porfiriato y la Revolución, 1898–1914.* Mexico City: Suprema Corte de Justicia de la Nación, 2010.

Rouaix, Pastor. *Génesis de los artículos 27 y 123 de la Constitución política de 1917.* 2nd ed. Mexico City: Talleres Gráficos de la Nación, 1959.

Ruíz, Ramón E. *The Great Rebellion: Mexico, 1905–1924.* New York: W. W. Norton, 1980.

Salamini, Heather Fowler. *Agrarian Radicalism in Veracruz, 1920–1938.* Lincoln: University of Nebraska Press, 1971.

Sayeg Helú, Jorge. *El constitucionalismo social mexicano: La integración constitucional de México, 1910–1917.* Mexico City: Cultura y Ciencia Política, 1974.

Serna de la Garza, José María. "The Concept of *Jurisprudencia* in Mexican Law." *Mexican Law Review* 1, no. 2 (2009): 131–45.

Sewell, William H., Jr. *Logics of History: Social Theory and Social Transformation.* Chicago: University of Chicago Press, 2005.

Silva Herzog, Jesús. *El agrarismo mexicano y la reforma agraria: Exposición y crítica.* 2nd ed. Mexico City: Fondo de Cultura Económica, 1964.

———. *Breve historia de la Revolución mexicana.* 2 vols. Mexico City: Fondo de Cultura Económica, 1969.

Spenser, Daniela. *The Impossible Triangle: Mexico, Soviet Russia, and the United States in the 1920s.* Durham, NC: Duke University Press, 1999.

———. *Stumbling Its Way Through Mexico: The Early Years of the Communist International.* Translated by Peter Gellert. Tuscaloosa: University of Alabama Press, 2011.

Suarez-Potts, William J. "The Mexican Supreme Court and the *Juntas de Conciliación y Arbitraje*, 1917–1924: The Judicialisation of Labour Relations After the Revolution." *Journal of Latin American Studies* 41 no. 4 (2009): 723–55.

Tannenbaum, Frank. *The Mexican Agrarian Revolution.* Washington, D.C.: Brookings Institution, 1930.

———. *Peace by Revolution: Mexico After 1910.* New York: Columbia University Press, 1929.

Tenorio Trillo, Mauricio, and Aurora Gómez Galvarriato. *El Porfiriato.* Mexico City: Fondo de Cultura Económica/Centro de Investigación y Docencia Económicas, 2006.

Toto, Mireya. *El amparo de la pequeña propiedad agraria.* Mexico City: Editorial Grijalbo, 1986.

Tutino, John. *From Insurrection to Revolution in Mexico: Social Bases of Agrarian Violence, 1750–1940.* Princeton, NJ: Princeton University Press, 1986.

Ulloa, Bertha. *La Constitución de 1917.* Historia de la Revolución mexicana, 6. Mexico City: Colegio de México, 1983.

Valadés, Diego. "Salvador Alvarado, un precursor de la Constitución de 1917." In *Estudios jurídicos en homenaje a don Santiago Barajas Montes de Oca*, 417–45. Mexico City: UNAM, 1975.

Valadés, José C. *El porfirismo: Historia de un régimen.* 3 vols. Mexico City: Robledo, 1941–1948.

Vazques Pérez, Francisco. "Régimen agrario." In *Evolución del derecho mexicano (1912–1942)*, vol. 1, 171–209. Mexico City: Editorial JUS, 1943.

Verner, Joel G. "The Independence of Supreme Courts in Latin America: A Review of the Literature." *Journal of Latin American Studies* 16 (1984): 463–506.

Wasserman, Mark. *Persistent Oligarchs: Elites and Politics in Chihuahua, Mexico, 1910–1940.* Durham, NC: Duke University Press, 1993.

Weber, Max. *Economy and Society: An Outline of Interpretative Sociology.* 2 vols. Edited and Translated by Guenther Roth and Claus Wittich. Berkeley: University of California Press, 1978.

Weldon, Jeffrey. "Political Sources of *Presidencialismo* in Mexico." In *Presidentialism and Democracy in Latin America*, edited by Scott Mainwaring and Mathew Soberg Shugart, 225–58. New York: Cambridge University Press, 1997.

Wiarda, Howard J. *The Soul of Latin America: The Cultural and Political Tradition.* New Haven, CT: Yale University Press, 2001.

Womack, John, Jr. "The Mexican Revolution, 1910–1920." In *Mexico Since Independence*, edited by Leslie Bethel, 125–200. Cambridge: Cambridge University Press, 1991.

———. *Zapata and the Mexican Revolution.* New York: Vintage Books, 1970.

Zamora, Stephen, José Ramón Cossío, Leonel Pereznieto, José Roldan-Xopa, and David López. *Mexican Law.* New York: Oxford University Press, 2004.

Index